ENJOY MOVING ABROAD

Three-Book Set of Insider Tips
for Living Well Overseas

Karen McCann

CAFÉ
SOCIETY
PRESS

Enjoy Moving Abroad:
Three-Book Set of Insider Tips for Living Well Overseas

Published by
Café Society Press
Hartland & Co.
1100 Superior Avenue East, Suite 700
Cleveland, OH 44114

ISBN 0-9850283-8-6

About the Resources Mentioned in the Text

References to useful websites and apps appear throughout the text. Don't worry, these are not sponsored ads or product placements. I never receive fees for mentioning goods, services, websites, or other resources, and I don't accept sponsorship of any kind. Every resource in this book (and in my other books, blog posts, and articles) is provided solely because I believe you might find it interesting and useful in planning your own adventures.

For my readers.

Thanks for joining us on the journey.

BOOKS BY KAREN MCCANN

MEMOIRS

Dancing in the Fountain
How to Enjoy Living Abroad

Adventures of a Railway Nomad
How Our Journeys Guide Us Home

TRAVEL & EXPAT GUIDES

Pack Light
*Quick & Easy Tips for Traveling Everywhere
with Just the Right Stuff*

How to Meet People on the Road
A Guide to Forming Friendships in Foreign Lands

101 Ways to Enjoy Living Abroad
Essential Tips for Easing the Transition to Expat Life

CONTENTS

101 Ways to Enjoy Living Abroad
Essential Tips for Easing the Transition to Expat Life

PACK LIGHT
Quick & Easy Tips for Traveling Everywhere with Just the Right Stuff

HOW TO MEET PEOPLE ON THE ROAD
A Guide to Forming Friendships in Foreign Lands

Look Inside
DANCING IN THE FOUNTAIN

BEFORE WE GET STARTED

For the first dozen years, whenever I told American friends that I'd moved from Cleveland, Ohio to Seville, Spain, I usually received indulgent smiles ("Of course you did! Who wouldn't, given the choice?") or the blank stares of those who clearly believed I was deranged ("Leave home? To live among strangers? Really? Why?"). But lately attitudes have changed. These days my email inbox is bristling with requests for practical information about how to leave the USA and settle overseas — preferably somewhere with congenial company, good weather, and affordable wine.

Living abroad has been wonderful for me, and I'm delighted to think the idea is catching on with a wider audience. Like most expats, I'm more than willing to pass along what I've learned about the process — which is a great deal more than I knew when I arrived in Seville with my husband and dog. In fact, ever since I moved to Spain in 2004, much of my writing life (to say nothing of my personal life) has been spent exploring topics I wish I'd been more savvy about from the beginning, such as how to get a residency visa, find a lost dog in an airport, and leave excess baggage — literal and figurative — behind. I started out writing about the practicalities and logistics but soon found myself addressing larger issues, such as how to create a new life from scratch, preferably one that's less frazzled, more authentic, and filled with generous amounts of friendship and laughter.

While you'll no doubt make friends with locals too, you'll likely find that the best place to jump-start your new social life is the international community. People living in a foreign country aren't surrounded by a network of relatives and lifelong friends, and they know that connecting with others takes time and effort. Many are extremely generous about reaching out to newcomers. They know just how strange it feels to wake up one morning in a new home in a new country with a calendar that's blank for the rest of your life. While this can be a trifle daunting at first, it's also tremendously liberating. You get to hit the reset button on your life. Whatever else you may be coping with, you certainly won't be stuck in a rut, operating on automatic pilot, wondering when the zing faded from your daily round.

Of course, relocating anywhere, even across your home town, has its challenges, and being in an unfamiliar culture speaking a foreign language doesn't make it any easier. At times you may feel as if you're a character in one of those old screwball comedies filled with absurd misunderstandings and general pandemonium. But no matter how zany the transition may get, you *will* eventually settle down — and that's when you're likely to start noticing how living abroad is enriching your life in a thousand ways you never dreamed possible.

Every expat journey begins with an online search, which is why I get so many query letters these days. It's impossible for me to answer every one in as much detail as I would like, so I decided to collect my three short guides into a single volume that offers potential expats a wide spectrum of handy tips, guidelines, and resources. And speaking of resources, this may be a good time to mention that I don't accept sponsorships or product placement of any kind, so the goods, services, websites, and other resources mentioned in these books are included solely because I thought you might find them useful in planning your own transition to expat life.

This collection begins with an overview of logistics and legalities in *101 Ways to Enjoy Living Abroad: Essential Tips for Easing the Transition to Expat Life*. Here you'll find simple guidelines that can help you decide whether, where, and how to make your move, enable you to avoid some pitfalls and cope with others, and give you the confidence you need to relax and enjoy the ride. You'll find suggestions for planning the move, house hunting, accessing health care, choosing a bank, tactfully evicting houseguests who have overstayed their welcome, making friends, dealing with culture shock, and learning the language (yes, you can!).

Expat life involves plenty of packing, not only when you're first heading overseas but later for visits back to the old country and for exploring your new country and the world at large. When it comes to hauling around possessions, our motto — and the title of the next guide in this series — is *Pack Light*.

My husband has spent decades working diligently (some might call it obsessively) on ways to whittle down the volume of our luggage without sacrificing comfort or functionality; I insist on maintaining some standards of stylishness as well. During more than three decades of marriage and visits to sixty-plus countries, Rich and I have learned a lot about what clothes are truly essential and which will sit at the bottom of the suitcase unworn. And while we have certainly bought plenty of gear over the years, we have finally mastered the art of resisting the latest "must have" travel gadgets we'll never use — and identifying those that are genuinely helpful. Don't worry, *Pack Light* doesn't suggest that you adopt a strictly minimalist approach, it simply provides ideas for gradually reducing the amount of excess baggage you're hauling around, so that your journeys become easier and more pleasant.

A few months ago, as I was being interviewed for a podcast, I was rambling on describing the benefits of traveling light and somehow got off on a tangent about memorable people I've met on the road — the friendly musicians in a Trieste dive bar, that dentist in Zagreb, and the Stockholm "oops" party. It was a morning interview and I was on my third cup of coffee, really picking up steam, when the interviewer finally managed to get a word in edgewise.

"Karen, how do you *meet* all these people?" she asked.

I get this question a lot, from both expats and general readers, and while I was answering the interviewer, half my mind was busy sketching out a plan for the third book in this collection, *How to Meet People on the Road: A Guide to Forming Friendships in Foreign Lands.* My original intent was to help travelers, but as I developed the book, I realized how valuable these tips are for those moving abroad, and I expanded the sections that are particularly relevant to the expat experience.

As you explore the question of whether and how to move overseas, I hope you'll find these tips helpful. Of course, my guides can't include every possible detail, and if there's a subject you feel needs to be explored further, or if you have resources or suggestions of your own to share, please let me know by writing to me at EnjoyLivingAbroad@gmail.com. I'm always looking for new material to cover on my blog and to include in future editions of this book.

And finally let me just say that moving abroad isn't as difficult, expensive, or challenging as many people think. Yes, it requires paperwork and packing, an investment of time and money, and the countless decisions that attend any transition. But look what you get for it: a new life filled with wonder.

I got my first taste of this kind of wonder when I was a child and my entire family gathered every year to watch the annual showing of the original 1939 *Wizard of Oz* on TV. The opening scenes, set in Kansas, are filmed in black and white. Then a tornado sends Dorothy's house flying, and after it lands there's this spectacular moment when she opens the door and discovers herself in the brilliant Technicolor world of Oz.

That moment inspired my lifetime of wanderlust. Arriving in a strange land often gives me that same feeling of jaw-dropping surprise and heart-lifting joy. No matter how many times I return to Seville after a visit to my native country, I always feel as if I'm stepping out of the airplane onto that yellow brick road, in giddy anticipation of astonishing adventures just ahead. May you feel that way about going abroad whenever you're lucky enough to do it.

101 WAYS
TO ENJOY LIVING ABROAD

Essential Tips for

Easing the Transition to Expat Life

101 Ways to Enjoy Living Abroad: Essential Tips for Easing the Transition to Expat Life

Published by
Café Society Press
Hartland & Co.
1100 Superior Avenue East, Suite 700
Cleveland, OH 44114

How To Feel at Home Wherever You Go

Want to learn how to feel at home in a foreign country, whether you're there for a weekend, a year, or a lifetime?

Fifteen years ago I was living in Ohio, following an early-to-bed, organic-vegetables-fresh-from-our-garden kind of lifestyle. It would never have occurred to me to have wine with lunch, take a siesta during the afternoon, or stay out until 2:00 in the morning — let alone finish up the night by walking home, arm in arm with friends, singing a medley of old show tunes, Beatles' hits, and *Bésame Mucho*. After moving to Seville, Spain, in 2004, I realized that spending time in a foreign country is an opportunity to reinvent yourself that rarely exists outside of the witness protection program. It's a fresh chance to build a new life that's authentically yours in a country that isn't.

This guide can help you decide whether, where, and how to make your move, enable you to avoid some of the pitfalls and cope with others, and give you the confidence that you need to relax and enjoy the ride.

And before we go any further, let me just say that while living in a foreign country has its challenges, it can be easier, more fun, and more affordable than you may think. You don't have to wait until all the stars are aligned, the dog passes away, the grandkids are grown, and you win the lottery. Bring the dog along (see Tips 23 to 31), expect frequent visits from family and friends, and don't worry about raising the kind of money you'd need to buy a Paris penthouse or restore a ruined castle in Scotland. Using a little common sense, and such money-saving suggestions as you'll find in this guide, your cost of living may actually go down or, as in my case, remain about the same as it was when I made my home in Cleveland.

While not every career can be uprooted and taken to another country, today many jobs can be managed online, and thanks to social networks, I am in closer contact with many of my loved ones than I was when we lived five minutes apart, or even in the same house. In fact, my initial concerns about missing family and friends evaporated when I learned that when you live abroad, especially in a destination city like Seville, *they* come to *you*. And before they do, you'll really want to review Tips 98 to 101 in the section Guests: Suggestions for Making Their Stay More Enjoyable (for You). Among other things, you'll learn tactful ways to dislodge guests who overstay their welcome and refuse to budge. (Yeah, I never thought it would happen to me either. Trust me, you'll want to be prepared for coping with this.)

Throughout *101 Ways to Enjoy Living Abroad*, I've included links to websites and references to products and services I thought you might find especially helpful. These links are not sponsored in any way; they are simply practical resources I've discovered and am passing along in hopes they will make your transition to expat life easier and less stressful.

In these pages you'll find the best strategies I've figured out, learned from experienced friends, or discovered the hard way, by doing the opposite and then having to sort out my mistakes. It covers the essentials I wish I'd known when I moved to Seville with my husband, Rich, and our dog, Eskimo Pie. In fact, I wish I'd been aware of these coping strategies before my shorter stays in other countries including Kenya, Thailand, Bhutan, El Salvador, Bosnia, and the Republic of Georgia. While this guide reflects my experiences as an American who moved to Spain, it's valid for anyone who is moving from one part of the world to another, and in many ways it applies to domestic relocations as well.

Living abroad can be enormous fun, and I hope this book makes it easier for you to navigate your transition and feel at home wherever you may find yourself.

Three Questions to Ask Before You Commit

1.

How much do you know about your potential new home? Online research is a great start; you may be surprised what you can learn on Wikipedia alone. Next, go for a visit. While this may not always be possible, today's low-cost air fares make it more feasible than ever, and it is a very sound investment in your future happiness. Ideally, go for several months and/or several visits; spend time exploring the town and the area. Just because you had a single, glorious weekend somewhere during spring break in college doesn't mean it's suitable for a business relocation, retirement, or year abroad with the family.

I've met disgruntled expats who moved to Seville on a whim and were subsequently shocked to discover that southern Spain isn't always sunny, we don't drink sangria with every meal, and while we are a very sociable town, not everybody can drop everything to meet you for a drink whenever you feel the urge. The more time you can spend getting to know a community, the more realistic you can be in evaluating its challenges and charms.

2.

If you are moving with a partner, do you both agree on the location? Dragging along a reluctant partner is no way to start a new life overseas. If both of you aren't equally keen on a particular destination, discuss why and see if accommodations can be made. One friend of mine dislikes commercial-laden Spanish network TV and for her, missing her favorite American shows was a major downside to the move. Today their household subscribes to every form of streaming available on the planet (see Tip 88 for more on this) and she happily escapes into the world of familiar entertainment on a regular basis.

3.

Why are you going? Is this the grand adventure you've always dreamed about? Are you moving for practical reasons, such as a lower cost of living or a healthier climate? Have you spent years longing to return to the scene of your finest youthful adventures? Do you have relatives in the area? This is a good time to take a clear-eyed look at your expectations and discuss them at length with anyone directly involved. Defining what you hope to achieve by this move will make it easier to make good decisions about it every step of the way.

THE PRE-DEPARTURE CHECKLIST

4.

Get a passport. As recently as 1990, only 10% of Americans held passports, but lately that number has risen to 43%, in part to comply with stricter travel laws that apply even to our nearest neighbors, Mexico and Canada. Already have a passport? Great! Now check the expiration date. Airlines won't let you fly from the USA to any overseas location if your passport isn't valid for at least 90 days. If you need to renew, you'll be glad to hear that US passport regulations now let you download the forms and renew by mail; expedited renewals are available for an extra fee.

5.

Apply for a residency visa. A residency visa is typically good for a year, where most tourist visas allow you to stay in a country for just 90 days. Residency visa regulations vary, so check the destination country's government web site for details. Most likely you'll need to start the application process in person at their embassy or consulate in your home country before you move. You will have to fill out a *lot* of forms and round up a thick stack of documents. When Rich and I applied for our Spanish residency visas, we had to attach proof of health insurance, bank statements, highlights of our investment portfolio, pension details, our Social Security benefits, a letter from our police chief confirming that we weren't wanted by any federal, state, county, or township law enforcement agencies, and a note from our doctor. "What, no epistle from the priest about how long it had been since our last confession?" said Rich. The process may continue for months after your arrival in your new home; by the time we got our paperwork sorted it was nearly time to file our applications for the following year. After the first year or two, renewals may become less frequent (often every two to five years) and more perfunctory.

6.

If vaccines are required or recommended, get them. Check with an online source such as the Centers for Disease Control Travelers' Health and then contact a travel clinic near you. These specialized clinics keep tabs on entry requirements, can provide any necessary vaccines and other medications, and will advise you about other sensible health precautions to consider (such as whether or not to drink the water). Find out if your immunization records will be accessible online; if not, be sure to bring a copy with you.

7.

Copy essential documents in case of loss. Make paper or electronic copies of your passport, credit cards, bank cards, insurance cards, and other all other cards you hold dear; in my case, this naturally included my library card for downloading free e-books (see tip 90). Copies can often be used to conduct business and will always be helpful in obtaining replacements should anything be lost or stolen. If you prefer paper copies, make two sets and keep them separate from the originals, and always in a carry-on bag or your pocket, not checked luggage.

When you're settled, find a safe place to store any originals that you won't need to access on a daily basis. After the second time my purse was snatched in Seville, I heeded a friend's advice and made a color copy my residency card and laminated it. Yes, I am carrying a fake ID. Would it fool officials at an international border? I doubt it. But it works fine for everyday needs, such as getting into museums for free and picking up packages from the post office.

8.

Notify your bank about your plans. You don't want them cancelling your credit and debit cards as soon as charges pop up in a new country.

9.

Set up on-line banking and bill paying. Your bank's website will walk you through the process so you can manage everything remotely. Eventually you may decide to close or transfer all your accounts, but most likely it will be more convenient to maintain them during the transition phase and possibly on an ongoing basis.

10.

Get a debit card if you don't have one. Unless you're in a very remote area, you'll find cash machines commonly available at banks and other locations. Ask about fees for using foreign cash machines; we've been charged as much as $15 for a single transaction. Find out if there's a way to avoid these fees by re-structuring your account or working with a different bank. Once you get settled, you'll open a local bank account, which should reduce your cash machine fees considerably.

11.

Inventory your electronic devices and upgrade any that are due for replacement in the next year. Yes, you can purchase computers, phones, and accessories overseas, but they are often more expensive, and foreign keyboards can have small but annoying differences. And yes, you can mail order them from your home country, but that adds shipping costs. Recharging cords, adaptors, and other accessories aren't as difficult to replace, but do an inventory and bring everything you're likely to need.

12.

Get an international driving permit. Valid in 150 countries, this permit basically translates your home country driver's license into nine languages and allows you to drive legally while you're abroad. US citizens over the age of 18 can apply by mail with the American Automobile Touring Alliance or in person or by mail with a local office of the American Automobile Association. The cost is around $20 and your permit is good for one year. Remember, if stopped by the police, you must be able to produce your home country driver's license as well as the international driving permit. In Spain, residents are required to get a local driver's license, which is an expensive, lengthy, and difficult process requiring a very good grasp of the language. Many expats don't comply with this law; some get away with it, others don't. A few years ago a friend was pulled over for speeding, and when she was extracting her US driver's license from her wallet, the officer noticed her residency card. Oops! Busted! She was banned from driving for a year (a huge problem for her commute to work) and then had to take an expensive course and an expensive exam to earn her Spanish license. Lesson learned: it pays to comply with local laws (or at least to avoid keeping your residency card where the cops can see it.)

13.

Have a complete physical before you move. You don't want any health surprises when you've just arrived in a new country. In the unlikely event that there is something that needs to be dealt with, you'll find it a lot easier in your home country and native language.

14.

Bring a good supply of your medications. Stock up to the greatest extent possible and if necessary, arrange to have someone collect your prescriptions and mail them to you. Give yourself time to get settled, then check whether your meds are sold over the counter. Even if they're not, in some countries, there's a certain latitude about prescriptions when dealing with foreigners; they assume you're a visitor who has run out and will often sell you a month's supply without a prescription. I bought one medication over the counter for more than five years before the pharmacist finally asked me to go to a local doctor and get a prescription so she could sell me my meds in complete compliance with the law.

15.

Arrange for your mail to be forwarded to you. File a change of address with the US post office in person or, if you don't mind paying a $1 fee, online. They'll forward first class mail for a year, periodicals and magazines for 60 days. Send your new address to everyone who is likely to mail you anything, such as the IRS, Social Security Administration, state election officials, and the billing department of your medical, dental, and other providers. If you're maintaining a place in your home country on an ongoing basis, arrange for someone to collect your mail and forward it to you. You may want a trusted friend or a virtual mailbox service to open your bills and letters, scan them, and email the scans to you; you'll get them faster and can always ask to have originals mailed to you if necessary.

16.

If you're keeping a place back home while living abroad, consider a house sitter and/or security system. You may need a full-time house sitter or simply someone to stop by regularly to check that everything is in order and confirm that scheduled maintenance, such as leaf removal or pest extermination, has been carried out. Leave a list of service providers in case any other home maintenance work is needed. A word of caution: teenage neighbors or relatives who are keen to take on the job may already be thinking of your place as party central. This is undesirable on so many levels. Make sure house sitters of any age are very clear on the parameters. And consider a security system with an alarm, possibly even surveillance cameras that send alerts and live-streamed video clips directly to your phone. You'll know instantly if thieves, beer-drinking teens, or anyone else is getting up to something in your absence.

ESSENTIAL PACKING TIPS

17.

Don't pack your entire wardrobe. There's an old saying that before you go on a trip, lay out all your clothes and all your money, then take half the clothes and twice the money. This goes double for moving overseas. You may not have a perfectly clear idea what you're likely to need in order to adapt to local weather conditions, social situations, and current fashion trends. It's best to arrive with an open attitude and room in your closet for a few additions.

18.

Bring along clothes that will help you fit in. At the time I moved to Seville, no one over the age of 18 ever appeared in the city wearing blue jeans, sneakers, or fleece tops; local women wore skirts or good slacks and shoes with heels. Having visited often before the move, I knew this and avoided showing up with my suitcase stuffed with things I'd never wear in public.

Luckily for me, Seville fashions have changed radically in the last five years, and now just about everyone is dressing in denim and sneakers; you even see fleece occasionally, and in hotter weather shorts are becoming more popular. But when I first arrived from rural Ohio, I made a lot of local purchases in an effort to fit in to my new environment — or at least not feel embarrassingly out of step with everyone around me.

19.

If you're crossing an ocean, don't ship furniture, cars, or other large items. I found it far more economical (and more fun) to furnish my apartment from scratch, shopping at Ikea for the big stuff and at funky boutiques to add touches of charm and originality. I once met two Americans who arrived in Spain with a car, masses of furniture, large kitchen appliances that were incompatible with local wiring systems, and a vague plan to open a B&B. This soon floundered, and last I heard they were heading back to the USA paying immense sums to ship all the stuff back.

20.

Take luggage you can manage by yourself. Rolling bags are a must, and you'll find two-wheelers are better on uneven pavements than the four-wheeled models. It's better to have two smaller bags than struggle to lug around something you can't heft or hoist; do not assume there will always be elevators, porters, or helpful bellhops when you need them.

21.

Keep items of vital importance (documents, medications, eyeglasses, Kindle, phone) in your carry-on. Never risk essentials in checked luggage that could be lost or delayed in transit.

22.

Carry all medications in their original containers. Not only can this help you get through customs, but it will make it easier for you to obtain replacements locally. Bring copies of all prescriptions, extra eyeglasses, and a first-aid kit.

TAKING ALONG YOUR PET

23.

Check your destination country's policy on pet immigration. An easy place to start is with an online resource such as PetTravel. Many countries don't require pets to be quarantined, so long as you have documents showing their health status and vaccination history; in some countries a microchip (see below) is also required. Collect all your pet's records in one file, sometimes referred to as a pet passport, which will be needed at customs and prove useful with your new veterinarian. If you're likely to be returning home with your pet at any point in the future, be sure to check on your own country's policies on admitting animals that have been overseas.

24.

Make sure your pet gets all needed vaccines and, if required, a microchip. Chips are small, about the size of a grain of rice, and our dog, Eskimo Pie, barely seemed to notice when the vet injected one in her shoulder. Be sure to get the appropriate chip; the entire world uses the ISO 15-digit microchips *except* for the USA, which uses a 9- or 10-digit chip which, thanks to proprietary encryption, cannot be read by international scanning machines. The good news is, you can now get ISO chips in the USA. This wasn't true some years back, so when we were bringing Pie to Spain, we had to drive her up to Canada have her international chip inserted. The fact she already had a US chip wasn't a problem; they simply injected the new one in the other shoulder.

25.

Research which airlines accept pets and have the best (and worst) reputation for pet safety. Pets fly safely every day — Pie did just fine in the cargo hold — but there are risks. Checking options for Pie's transport, I phoned Iberia, the Spanish airline. "You're bringing your *dog*?" the woman who answered asked incredulously. "Can't you leave it at home? It's not good for dogs to travel by air. They're cold, they're frightened, they're upset, they get sick, they get loose, they get out on the runway, they get killed..." Yikes! Obviously we chose another airline. And — let me say again — she made it through the journey with flying colors.

26.

Consider having your pet declared an emotional support animal (ESA). Small pets can travel in the main cabin, and so can larger animals if the owners get a letter from a mental health professional declaring the pet an emotional support animal. If you don't have a mental health professional in your life, there are online services that will provide such letters for a fee.

Some friends who are about to make the move to Spain have had their dog declared an ESA and have already bought an extra seat so he can ride in comfort on the plane. They're also bringing along two cats in the cabin and have enlisted a friend to come along as a "cat escort" to make sure there are enough humans to keep the pets organized, happy, and safe.

27.

If you'll be staying in a hotel, Airbnb, or other temporary lodgings, check pet policies in advance. Many will accept pets but often have restrictions about size, certain breeds, and supervision, and they may require that you pay a special fee or deposit.

28.

Check apartment pet policies before you rent. Just days before moving in to our Seville apartment, after we'd bought all the furniture and major appliances and arranged for their delivery, we learned that our landlord had a no-pets policy (which is very rare in this part of Spain). We had to do some fast talking to get special permission for Pie to move in.

Later we learned that most Sevillanos blithely ignore such policies; the couple in the apartment next to us just got a dog and certainly never informed the landlord or asked permission. But as newcomers who didn't know how seriously the no-pets clause would be viewed, we were happier to jump through the hoops rather than worry about losing our lease or spending years sneaking Pie in and out of the building.

29.

Find a veterinarian as soon as possible. Just like humans, pets can arrive feeling discombobulated by the move and may show physical or mental signs of distress, including acting out in strange ways. If your animal companion seems to be having trouble adjusting, look around your new neighborhood, ask others who are walking their dogs in the park for advice, or go online to find an expat club and post the question on their website.

30.

As a guest in the country and a responsible pet owner, you'll want always to be equipped to clean up after your pet. As posters for a public campaign in Seville put it, "Please pick up after your dog until he can do it for himself."

31.

If you're a dog owner, find the parks or trails where your neighbors like to walk their pets. Like you, your dog needs to make new friends and have time for socializing. Don't be surprised if it takes considerably longer for you to make friends with the humans on the other end of the leash.

When You Arrive

32.

Mentally unpack your bags. Accept that this is home, and make an effort to, as the Buddhists put it, "be here now." It's natural to look back on your old life, but try not to dwell on it 24/7. Look around, focus on what's happening in your current environment, and (to the greatest extent possible) accept your new life on its own terms.

33.

Reset your watch to local time; your internal clock will soon follow. Try to avoid the temptation to say things like, "Back home right now it's four o'clock in the morning," which will just make you feel more tired and disoriented.

34.

Assume everything will be different. You'll be pleasantly surprised when you discover things that are like home.

Traveling with Kids

35.

You'll need a passport for each child. Learn details of the application process by consulting official websites; US residents can start with the State Department's page about travel with children under 16, there's another page for children 16 to 17. Both parents or guardians must authorize the issuance of a child's passports, and both are asked to go with the child in person to submit the application. Government websites define exceptions and workarounds that can be made if both parents or guardians cannot be present.

36.

Bring copies of the child's birth certificate. This is especially important if there is more than one surname in the family. If applicable, you'll also need a Consular Report of Birth Abroad, a foreign birth certificate, and/or an adoption decree.

37.

If you're divorced and the child is under a custody arrangement, bring copies of the divorce degree and custody papers. In some countries, you may need a notarized letter from an absent spouse giving permission for you to travel with the child. Find out what's required in every country you may be passing through.

38.

Get kids any recommended vaccinations. You'll want to be very sure your child is completely up to date with all the usual inoculations plus whatever is recommended for areas you'll be traveling through or living in (see Tip 6). If you happen to be in an area experiencing an outbreak or epidemic, it's vital to be able to show health officials what your child has been inoculated against. In any case, you'll want the records handy so you can provide your new pediatrician with details of your child's health status.

39.

Bring some entertainment for your child. In addition to electronic devices with movies, games, and music, consider such old-school entertainment as books, playing cards, Legos, or coloring books (be sure to pack crayons). Older kids may enjoy a camera, sketch pad, journal, or a smartphone or tablet that's equipped with an app such as iMovie they can use to record and present their impressions of the trip.

40.

If you're traveling with infants and toddlers, pack three or four days' supply of diapers, formula, wipes, etc.. Unless you're going to a very remote wilderness location, you'll soon be able to re-stock at the local pharmacy or grocery store, but it helps have enough on hand for the trip and a day or two besides.

41.

Bring water and packaged snacks on the plane. Toddlers, some older children, and let's face it, many adults will appreciate graham crackers, granola bars, or other familiar snacks as a break from constantly sampling foreign cuisine during the trip and early transition days.

Once you're settled, find out where you can get familiar international foods in your new home city. Check to see if there's a Taste of America shop near you; they charge a premium, but you may find the extra cost is worth it to give your family name brand products from home, at least until they're feeling a bit less discombobulated.

42.

Prepare your children psychologically for the changes they'll experience. Talk to them about the differences to expect in their new environment (such as meal and school schedules) and make sure they have the chance to say their goodbyes to friends and places they'll miss.

43.

Before you go, check out schools in your new community. Useful online resources include International Schools Review and the US State Department's Worldwide Schools. Find out how far in advance you have to register; it may be considerably sooner than you'd think.

After you arrive in your new home country, talk to other parents, especially expats, to get a more nuanced understanding of local options. Your online choice may not be your final one, but having some advance knowledge will make it easier to look forward rather than back, and may help you avoid having to scramble to get your kids placed at the last minute.

44.

Encourage kids to learn the language and try new things. When they get frustrated or homesick, be patient and allow them time to adapt. Good descriptions of the stages of culture shock and coping strategies may be found on blogs such as Expat Child and Multicultural Kids.

HOUSE HUNTING

45.

Consider renting rather than buying. It's smart to avoid being locked in before you've really had a chance to explore the various neighborhoods, learn about local real estate values, and discover whether your new home is a good long-term fit. You may find (as Rich and I did) that it makes more economic sense, and is far less hassle, to continue renting indefinitely. In addition to short-term practical considerations, such as how willing/able you are to deal with repair people in a foreign language, there can be financial risk and significant estate and tax consequences. On the plus side, in 30 countries home ownership guarantees a foreign passport or at least an elite residency status. Until you're up to speed on all the options and issues, it pays to rent, at least temporarily.

46.

Check out local housing prices in advance. Read online listings and contact real estate agents, but avoid making a long-term commitment without seeing the place in person. Airbnb has changed the rental landscape in many cities, taking an ever-larger portion of long-term rental properties off the market and upping the sophistication of the way places are photographed and shown online. We've all been surprised when the hotel that appeared so glamorous in the Internet photos turned out to be a dive in a ghastly neighborhood. Where you live is a decision you don't want to repent at leisure.

47.

In deciding between country, suburbs, and city, consider your personality and lifestyle. If you like peace and quiet, a rural setting may be perfect. If you feel a garden is a must, especially with kids, the suburban lifestyle may be for you. If social and cultural activities are a priority, and you prefer walking to driving, then you might want an apartment in the city.

I'm often baffled by the fact that so many Americans assume rural life will be easier and more rewarding. Apparently reading *A Year in Provence* leaves the indelible impression that nothing beats moving to a tiny European village and spending years renovating a crumbling farmhouse with the help of colorful local characters who will share earthy wisdom and great recipes.

Most people I know who have moved to a European village find it hideously isolating. It's not easy to live in place where no one speaks your language and everyone else has known one another since baptism. My friends usually decide to leave, then struggle through a long period of intense frustration trying to sell their house. As mentioned above, it pays to rent and get a feel for what your life is actually going to be like in any community you're considering.

48.

Before you rent or buy, check out the neighborhood. Are there sufficient markets and shops nearby? Too many noisy bars? Great museums and concert halls? Your kids' school? A meth lab? You want to feel safe and have the activities of daily living within easy reach.

49.

Review the lease or purchase agreement with someone who speaks the language and knows local real estate. Dealing with legalese in a foreign language is tricky at best; it pays to get professional help.

Banking Basics

50.

Set up an account with a local bank. Even if you've got online banking in your home country, there are likely to be times when you need a local account, for instance to reduce fees on cash withdrawals or to make automatic payments to your landlord and the utility companies.

Be prepared for surprises, such as very different policies regarding interest or convoluted methods for transferring money. And watch out for changes; one day I went to a cash machine and discovered that our inexpensive withdrawals suddenly cost 12€ per transaction. This was because the local banks had decided to restructure their fees to be more attractive for people making automatic monthly payments from a salary or pension. Not having either of these income streams making deposits to our Spanish account, we were forced to pay ridiculous new fees until we found a Dutch bank with a more conventional fee structure. It pays to do the legwork to find the right bank.

51.

Consider using a transfer company rather than having a bank move your money overseas. If you will be making transfers from your home country to your new bank, take a hard look at the costs. Most banks give an unfavorable currency conversion rate, charge a markup, and add a fee on top of that. This is a costly way to shift money around. Many expats prefer to work with a reputable transfer company such as TransferWise.

LEARNING THE LANGUAGE

52.

Take classes. Unless you're an extraordinarily gifted linguist, you won't pick up a working knowledge of a language from hanging around listening to people use it in cafés and markets. Yes, I know, toddlers do it all the time — but do you really want to talk like a toddler? You need to learn the rules, masses of vocabulary, and tricks for committing it all to memory. True, it might be possible to survive speaking nothing but English, but you will miss out on so much of the fun if you do. Get started on your language studies as soon as possible.

53.

Take private classes if you can afford them. Your learning rate will skyrocket. And a private teacher can work with subjects that interest you (local culture, hobbies, food) or that you'll need, such as vocabulary related to your job, the kids' school, or that persistent plumbing issue in the downstairs bath.

Rich and I arranged to have our Spanish teacher take us on long walks through the city one afternoon every week, discussing what we were seeing and helping us translate signs and menus. It was fun, really helped us understand the city, and gave us some seriously practical vocabulary (plus a bit of exercise as an added bonus).

54.

Give it time. If you're over thirty, you'll likely need months for the basics, years to become fluent, a lifetime to work on your accent. Keep at it; the more you know of the language, the more enjoyable and comfortable your life will become. It truly is worth the effort. And remember, making "stupid" mistakes is part of the learning process. Not long after we arrived in Seville, Rich wanted to make a small repair in our apartment. After a quick trip to the dictionary, we set out for the hardware store muttering to ourselves *"destornillador, destornillador, destornillador"* (screwdriver, screwdriver, screwdriver). Unfortunately, when we arrived, my mind went blank and Rich blurted out a similar word, *ordenador* (computer), causing such mutual confusion that we were forced to abandon the attempt and flee the scene without buying either a screwdriver or a computer. We were pretty flustered and annoyed with ourselves at the time, but when we calmed down, we had a good laugh and have been telling that story for years. Our Spanish has improved considerably, but we still flounder sometimes, and when that happens, I find that most people appreciate that you're making an effort and will do their best to help the conversation along.

55.

Brush up on your charades skills. Sometimes a bit of pantomime will help you over the sketchy parts of your vocabulary. Here in Seville, when you're ready for your bill in a café, it's common simply to mime the act of writing, which expats love as it puts off the day they actually have to remember how to say *"la cuenta."*

Culture Shock and Homesickness

56.

Try to view differences as just differences. They are not a commentary on you, your decision to move, the country in which you find yourself, your ability to adapt, or the entire trajectory of your life.

57.

Avoid endless comparison to the old country. Naturally, similarities and differences will spring to mind — a lot — but if you can only view the present through a constant overlay of the past, it will make it much harder to build a better future in your new home.

58.

Accept that you will always stand out as a foreigner. That's especially true in a place as steeped in tradition as southern Spain, where most people spend their entire life socializing with neighbors they've known since birth. You can never join that inner circle, but you can be part of the community and make a place for yourself that's uniquely your own and richly rewarding. You may encounter locals who are too uncomfortable with anything unfamiliar to befriend anyone new. But you'll meet others who will go out of their way to engage with you because you're different and interesting. Enjoy those friendships.

59.

Don't ignore feeling blue, alienated, or homesick. Moving throws you off balance; accept this as natural and apply home remedies. Mine include dark chocolate, French wine, and lighthearted movies. A few days of this regimen can go a long way toward restoring emotional equilibrium. If you can't shake the blues, consider therapy or determine whether it's time to make some changes in your life.

Making Friends

60.

When you're new in town, be open to all social opportunities. If someone suggests getting together to attend an art exhibit, sporting event, or even a bullfight, give it careful consideration, regardless of whether you like impressionist paintings, soccer, or watching animals be killed. You need to get out there and meet people; say "yes" whenever you can. Obviously invitations to participate in crimes, skullduggery, and/or undesirable sexual liaisons should be politely declined.

61.

Remember your manners. You're a guest in another country and need to abide by its laws and show respect for its norms and customs. For instance, if you live in a country where smoking is legal and common, it's rude as well as pointless to go around — as one expat I knew used to do — harassing people for lighting up in bars. It certainly didn't get anyone to smoke less, nor did it improve their opinion of US standards of courtesy or common sense.

On countless occasions I have been the first American someone from another country has ever spent time with, and my words and actions reflect on my entire nation. The USA is the focus of enough international controversy these days; I don't want to add to it.

62.

Bear in mind that the locals don't want to hear constant comparisons between your county and theirs. They especially don't want to hear unfavorable comparisons. Most people identify strongly with their birthplace and do not take kindly to hearing it criticized for being less [*fill in the adjective of your choice*] than the town you grew up in.

If you must draw comparisons, find a way to complement your new home and how it functions. For instance, I make sure to let my Spanish doctors know how impressed I am with the efficiency of the clinic I go to, which usually gives me same-day appointments, rarely makes me wait more than ten minutes, and sends me in directly to see the doctor, without all that fussing about getting into gowns and being weighed by a nurse. Frankly, if I'm there for a persistent cough, I don't think any of us really cares whether I've gained or lost a pound or two. My point is that I can honestly make a favorable comparison, which I find always goes down well.

63.

Your new friends and neighbors will probably have limited interest in your travels. Most will become jealous and/or bored if you go on and on about all the cool places you've visited that they will never see. Try a different approach.

Ask about local places of interest, such as nearby archeological sites or beaches; find out if they have recommendations about monuments and restaurants you should visit. You'll get good advice and they will have the satisfaction of displaying insider knowledge of the region.

64.

Accept local attitudes towards punctuality and other social niceties. In some countries, being an hour late for a lunch date is considered normal and nothing to get upset about. Find out about local norms and plan your social life accordingly. For example, include a few punctual Brits or Americans among your lunch guests so you'll have someone to talk to while you're waiting for the others to arrive.

65.

Be open to new friends of all ages. America is more rigidly stratified along generational lines than any other country I know. When you live in a community with a small international population, you can't afford to place arbitrary limitations on your circle of friendship. If people share your language, interests, and sense of humor, do you really care how old they are or what nation they were born in? Our friends range from 20 to 84 and come from Europe, Asia, New Zealand, Latin America, the UK, and the USA; that keeps the conversation lively.

66.

Consider joining a social club or engaging in communal activities. Even if you're not normally much of a joiner, signing up for a cooking course, painting class, or bicycling group can be a great way to meet locals. Consider joining the free expat social network InterNations, which has over three million members in 420 cities around the world and regularly organizes informal gatherings such as pub nights, hiking, and dinners. For more options, Google social clubs in your area.

67.

Don't isolate yourself. Sometimes living abroad feels overwhelming, and we all have days when we want to stay home and pull the covers over our heads. That's natural and fine to do once in a while, when you really need to catch your breath. But the more you can get out and interact with your new world, the sooner it will start feeling like home.

Working

68.

You'll need a work visa. If you're moving overseas for a job, the human resources staff of your company will likely take care of getting the visa for you; ask them to obtain visas for your partner/family as well. If you have a residency visa, you may be prohibited from working. However, if the right job opportunity comes up, your new employer may be able to help you obtain a work visa. And after a number of years living in the country, you may be automatically granted the right to work as part of your residency visa; this happened to us somewhere around year seven.

69.

Have a qualified professional review all contracts before you sign them. Even if the contract is "just routine" employment paperwork, you'll want someone with a firm grasp of the language and legal implications to confirm that this contract says what you think it says. Contact your home country's consular office or embassy to get a list of English-speaking lawyers in your area.

70.

Learn local business customs. Don't assume that everyone has the same attitude toward, for instance, payment schedules and work hours. In Seville, I know savvy local businesspeople who have waited years for contracts to be honored and payments to be rendered. Spend time talking to others in your company, your field, and the international community to find out what to expect.

71.

Research the business culture. The book *Kiss, Bow or Shake Hands: The Bestselling Guide to Doing Business in More than 60 Countries* outlines business etiquette around the world. Good online references include The Culture Crossing Guide and Cultural Atlas. These insider tips can help you avoid countless missteps in the workplace (and in your social life).

72.

Be prepared for resentment. Any foreigner who is hired, especially for a desirable management position, is likely to inspire jealousy and hostility, especially from local employees who had their eye on the job. Try not to take it personally and be sure to watch your back.

73.

Consider working online. How? One way to do this is to check the international listings on Craigslist. I know an American couple who came to Seville in 2008 for jobs that didn't work out, so they went on Craigslist and found online employment in sales and marketing. They now conduct all their business online and via phone using Skype with a US number (which clients tend to find reassuring). Their home base is now in New Zealand, but they continue to travel extensively, working as they go and exploring the world in their off hours.

Eat, Drink, and Be Merry

74.

Eat the local food. OK, you don't have to order the fried flies in Bangkok or the snake stew in Hanoi, but give the mainstream regional offerings a chance. You may be delightfully surprised. Among my favorites in Spanish cuisine are such unlikely traditional dishes as pig cheeks, tail of the bull, and various shellfish that look like alien life forms. Even if you don't like what you've ordered — for instance, I recently learned to my dismay that Portuguese pig's ears are just as tasteless and rubbery as you'd expect — you get a good story out of it.

75.

Drink what the locals drink. Here's an opportunity to practice the art of letting go of old habits that can no longer be indulged. The local café doesn't serve your favorite white mocha frappuccino dusted with cinnamon? Find out what drinks they do offer and start sampling until you discover something you enjoy. Yes, I miss the buttery chardonnay of my native California, but in Seville's hot climate, it's more sensible to drink beer or a *tinto de verano* (summer red wine), which is iced red wine mixed with a fizzy soft drink. Bartenders are usually happy to describe what's available and identify what other people around you are ordering. This will also give you a chance to practice your linguistic skills and pick up useful vocabulary. Insider tip: Many people find speaking a foreign language becomes much easier after a few beers or glasses of wine. Just saying.

76.

Adapt to local eating schedules. Eating is part of your social life as well as your nutritional intake for the day. Visitors who arrive in Seville and insist on eating lunch at noon and dinner at 7:00 pm, as they would back home, can only go to touristy, corporate-run places; traditional venues offer meals at traditional times, close for siesta, and don't re-open for dinner until at least 8:30 pm. Eating alone in a tourist trap isn't nearly as much fun, or as culturally interesting, as exploring the city's restaurant scene.

77.

You may have to work a bit harder to accommodate special dietary needs abroad. That said, gluten-free, vegetarian, even vegan options are now being offered at many traditional restaurants all over the world. Use your online translator to compile some key phrases explaining what you're looking for and what you need to avoid. At first you may want to write out key phrases in large, clear letters you can show the waiter, rather than struggling with the pronunciation or asking harried staff to squint at your phone's tiny screen to figure out what you're talking about.

78.

Throw a party. Even if you're still working out all the nuances of entertaining in the local style, invite people over for dinner. I've learned that most people are fascinated by the American

Thanksgiving feasts they've seen in the movies, and few will pass up an opportunity to experience this exotic ritual for themselves. You may have to make special arrangements to buy a whole turkey from the poultry market, and pay staggering prices for cans of cranberry sauce and pumpkin at shops catering to foreigners, but it's a fun way to entertain. In the spirit of the holiday (even if we're holding the party at another time of year) we ask everyone to take turns standing up and describing something they are thankful for. Getting people gathered around a dinner table and talking about themselves is a great way to foster friendships.

TRANSPORTATION OPTIONS

79.

Walking is the most practical way to get around cities and town centers. Many old cities have labyrinthine historical districts with nightmarish traffic patterns and no place to park. Even some small towns can pose challenges. Early in our time in Spain, Rich rented a car to drive some visitors to a mountain village. As we entered, some old men sitting in the main plaza waved and shouted, *"Estrecho! Estrecho!"* I had a vague feeling we'd covered that vocabulary word in class but didn't recall that it meant "narrow" until our vehicle was actually wedged firmly between two stone walls at a bend in the ever-skinnier back lanes. When we eventually, with considerable shrieking of metal and loss of paint, managed to extricate ourselves, we went back to the plaza and noticed the large sign telling everyone to park there and walk.

We now take such signs seriously. And even when we're not in tight places, we have embraced walking as our preferred form of exercise. It's a great way to become acquainted with a new community and enjoy some aerobic activity — to say nothing of the cost savings, including parking fees and car repairs.

80.

Bicycling is often a practical alternative. Many European cities have municipal bikes you can rent for a modest fee, picking them up and leaving them in public lots all over town. This is a great first step, even if you intend to purchase one of your own. You'll learn how practical it is to bike through the city's traffic patterns to key destinations, and should the bike be stolen (sadly, an all-too-common occurrence) you won't have to bear the financial loss.

81.

Explore the public transportation system. Buses, subways, and trains are often the cheapest and most convenient way to get around. Cities tend to have vast transportation networks while rural and suburban areas may have limited service. Find out what's offered in your area and take excursions to learn the system. Many Americans assume they need a car to survive anywhere and may be pleasantly surprised to learn they don't.

82.

Find out about ridesharing, car sharing, and rentals. City dwellers will want to take a hard look at the cost of buying, maintaining, insuring, and garaging a vehicle vs. using a ridesharing service such as Uber, joining a car-sharing program such as Zipcar or Hertz 24/7, or renting a car when needed. Unless you require daily use of a car for purposes such as commuting to work or driving kids to a distant school, you're likely to find you really do not need a car of your own on a full-time basis.

83.

Research local requirements for leasing or purchasing a car. If you live in the suburbs or country, or must drive long distances regularly for work or family reasons, you'll likely find driving a car the most practical option. Find out about local options for leasing vs buying, and ask co-workers, friends, and/or a lawyer what kind of paperwork is required. Be extremely careful, especially if buying a used vehicle, to make sure it is really transferred to your name and that everything's in order.

Keep in Touch

84.

Adapt your smartphone or buy a go-phone. Check the purchase paperwork or ask your provider to determine whether your smartphone is locked (usable only with your original provider) or set up for international use. Recent iPhones, for instance, now have a SIM card slot that's unlocked so you can simply buy a SIM card in your new home country and insert it. If your phone isn't unlocked, you can pay a service to do this for you once you arrive.

Not a smartphone person? Buy a "go phone," an inexpensive local mobile that lets you pay for calls or other functions as you use them, without a contract or monthly fees. Once you have a feel for your usage pattern, an annual contract may prove more economical.

If you're not into Texting or WhatsApp, you probably will be; they're the major form of communication in many countries, with actual phone calls becoming increasingly rare. For more technical details, consult articles such as *TripSavvy*'s "How to Use Your Smartphone Overseas."

85.

Sign up for Skype. If you're not already using this low-cost internet-based phone service, now's the time to check it out. Calls to other users are free and for a modest fee you can make low-cost calls to non-members' mobiles and landlines. The video option (which you can switch off if you're still in your pajamas) lets you talk face to face with other Skype users. For long-distance business and personal calls, it's a great way to go. Other video calling apps include Facebook Messenger, Google Duo, and Apple's FaceTime, but Skype remains the industry standard.

86.

Use social media to stay connected. Even if you're not a fan of Facebook, Twitter, and other social media outlets, they offer an easy way to stay connected with family, friends, colleagues, and world events. If you haven't already taken the plunge, this is probably a good time to sign up for one or more of these free services. Facebook is a good place to start, I find ads on social media incredibly annoying, so I was delighted to discover that, as a Google Chrome user, I could use their free AdBlock, which means I never see ads on Facebook.

Rich has an even better approach. Some glitch on Facebook resulted in his birthdate being listed as 1907, at which point the advertising community figured he wouldn't live long enough to make any more purchases, so they stopped sending ads his way. Rich is a minimalist user, but I like Facebook and use it to maintain ongoing conversations with people all over the world. If you are jumping in for the first time, come visit my EnjoyLivingAbroad Facebook page and say hi!

ENTERTAINMENT

87.

Don't expect outstanding local TV in every country. Spanish TV, for instance, is so heavily laced with commercials at seemingly random intervals that I can't seem to keep track of the storyline of the show. This isn't helped by the fact that the only time I watch local TV is when I'm in a bar. But even when I'm there sipping a coffee, I generally find Spanish TV confusing and unsatisfying. Some of the best entertainment comes from the commercials, which are far more outrageous than US TV allows. But there are better options (see below) for enjoying mass media and practicing your new language.

88.

Sign up for a VPN to stream movies and TV shows. Subscription services such as Netflix and Amazon Prime are regionally coded, which (theoretically) means you can only use them in the country where you enrolled. Luckily they're now available in many parts of the world, so often you can simply set up a new account in your new home. However, if they're not available in your area, or you want to continue using your American account for a while, you can, for a modest monthly fee, contract with a Virtual Private Network. A VPN fools your computer into thinking you are in the USA (or whatever country you designate), so you can access your American accounts and watch the new season of *Stranger Things* or *Sneaky Pete* the minute it comes out. At first I was convinced this had to be illegal, but everything I've Googled says VPNs are allowed in most countries and regions, including the Americas, Europe, Australia, and Africa.

If you don't have an entertainment account such as Netflix or Amazon Prime, or want to watch a show that isn't included in your subscription service, you can rent or buy individual movies and TV shows on Amazon; there is no regional coding standing in the way of a direct purchase. Superhot, first run movies are expensive, but most shows are modestly priced. For free entertainment, YouTube offers lots of older movies as well as contemporary comedy, music, TED Talks, cooking videos, and other programming.

89.

Connect your TV to your computer. If you're streaming movies and TV shows, you may want to buy a TV and connect it to your computer so you can watch on a bigger screen. Choose a TV that's pre-wired for this; an HDMI port lets you run a cable between your TV and your computer. We have now reached the absolute limits of my technical knowledge on this subject; if you want more, there's a WikiHow article called "How to Connect PC to TV" that spells it out in full.

90.

If you like books, get an e-reader such as Kindle. Yes, I know, an e-reader doesn't have the comfy feel of a traditional book. But let's face it, unless you're in a country that speaks English, you're not going to have a huge selection of "real" books around, and mail ordering gets expensive fast. I resisted for a while, and when I finally gave in and bought a Kindle, it took me about fifteen minutes to get used to it. Now I prefer it, because I can control the size of the type, carry the slim little thing with me anywhere (try doing that with a hardbound copy of *War and Peace*), and look up words I don't know (including having Spanish translations at a tap of my finger). I also love the way online retailers let you download a free sample of any book you're considering; if you like it, you can purchase the e-book in seconds from anywhere in the world.

Most American public libraries let you remotely download books for free; if you don't have a library card, get one and find out how to go about downloading books, audio books, and more. Online retailers such as Amazon have for-pay subscription services that make thousands of books available at no additional charge. If you are a voracious reader like me, you will definitely want an e-reader while you are abroad.

91.

Check out podcasts on the Internet. If you miss radio, podcasts are a great way to keep current on news and culture. You can click and play, or download them for later. Some are free, such as many of the NPR and BBC shows, while other sources, such as the Apple iTunes store, charge a fee.

92.

Remember that not all entertainment involves an electronic device. Tourist offices and local publications can provide information about guided and self-guided tours, local points of interest, concerts, exhibitions, children's activities, and more. Some cultures (yes, Seville, I am talking about you!) don't always feel compelled to maintain strictly accurate online information, so try not to be too surprised if the concert starts a half hour later than advertised, or the cost is eight euros instead of five, or the museum closes for a holiday you've never heard of. Try to maintain a relaxed attitude and have a fallback plan in mind.

HEALTH CARE

93.

Make sure you have sufficient medical insurance. If necessary, purchase additional coverage in your new country. For Americans retiring abroad, it's important to know that Medicare does not cover you outside of the USA. If you live in a country with universal health care, you won't qualify for it unless you are a taxpaying citizen. My husband and I have US insurance plus some modestly priced private insurance from a Spanish provider; this entitles us to go to private clinics with much faster service and, if necessary, to have a doctor visit us at home. Yes, that's right, they make house calls! In many countries they're routine — and a lifesaver if you're really ill.

94.

Find out the location of the nearest and best hospitals and clinics. Do an Internet search, then check with friends, your landlord, and/or the local pharmacy to identify the ones you'll want to use. If you need an English-speaking physician, often the embassy or consular office will have a list of those in your area.

95.

The local pharmacy is often your best access to the health care system. Pharmacists are trained to provide medical advice and, in many places, can sell you medications over the counter that would require a prescription back home. I took a US visitor with back problems to my neighborhood pharmacy and explained that his doctor, consulted by email, had recommended Prednisone. My friend was sure this would involve an expensive doctor's visit and costly drugs, and he was stunned when pharmacy supplied precisely what he needed at a cost of $3.75.

In our neighborhood, you often have the added benefit of advice from other customers, who are only too happy to chime in with tips and stories about how Aunt Maria cured her kid's ear infection with half an onion placed beside the bed at night. (Yes, of course I tried this, and yes, it does help a little, but it's no substitute for ibuprofen.)

96.

Don't be surprised if your doctor or pharmacist recommends a homeopathic treatment. In Europe, 40% of physicians either prescribe homeopathic remedies or refer people to practitioners in the field; it's integrated into the national health care systems of Germany, France, Switzerland, the United Kingdom, Greece, Israel, India, Pakistan, and Mexico, to name but a few. If you're not familiar with it, do a bit of research (Wikipedia is a good place to start) so you'll be familiar with the concept if a homeopathic approach is suggested.

While some medical practitioners, especially in the USA, are skeptical or downright hostile to this practice, I've successfully used homeopathic remedies — including my favorite No-Jet-Lag — for many years. Some of those skeptics claim it's simply the placebo effect. Do I care, so long as it works?

Have a "Plan B." If you don't feel confident about the quality of medical treatment available or your ability to access appropriate care due to language difficulties or highly specialized needs, consider regular visits to your country of origin (or another country in which you have confidence) for health maintenance.

Back in the 1990s, Rich and I were working with a group of doctors in the Republic of Georgia, which in those days had a very fragile medical infrastructure. After a tour of a hospital damaged by an earthquake, where the staff was attempting to care for patients in a facility lacking electricity, food, water, medications, heat, and, in many areas, glass in the windows, one of our clients said, "Don't worry, if you ever needed medical care, we would fly you to Turkey." This was not quite as reassuring as hearing we'd be flown to the Mayo Clinic, but we appreciated the thought. That's when we first started considering emergency medical evacuation insurance, and depending on where you're going, you might want to look into this as well.

Guests: How to Make Their Stay More Enjoyable (for You)

98.

There are two types of guests: the independent ones and those who need a *lot* of handholding. You may not be able to identify them in advance; little old ladies who have never been out of the village of Chagrin Falls, Ohio can prove far more fearless than strapping ex-Marines.

99.

Be clear up front about the duration of their stay. Twice I've had people arrive for a weekend and stay nearly two weeks. Vague mutterings about moving on never amounted to anything, and our subtle hints (bringing home brochures for nearby cities they'd intended to visit) were utterly ignored. They kept telling us how much fun they were having and asking whether we minded if they stayed on another day or two. Raised with strict notions of hospitality, Rich and I were simply unable to throw them bodily into the street.

Nowadays, when people let us know they're contemplating a visit, we're careful to say that if their visit is likely to last more than a few days, they will probably be more comfortable in a nearby hotel or Airbnb. We're happy to offer the names of websites offering a range of accommodations.

100.

Do a little pre-trip planning with your guests-to-be. If they will be staying with you, describe the accommodations; for example, let them know if there's no TV or if they will be sleeping on a couch or inflatable mattress. Tell them about local conditions, for instance that almost no one speaks English and everything will be closed for siesta in the middle of the day. Suggest that they do online research and come up with things they'd like to do on their own. Explain that while they are on vacation, you are not, and although naturally you'll want to spend time with them, you will have other obligations to fulfill during their stay. Of course, some guests will ignore all of this and require considerable maintenance during their stay. Your only recourse at that point is to take care of them with whatever grace you can muster.

Or try the handy trick described below.

101.

Here's one way to dislodge of a house guest who refuses to leave. One friend of mine was unable to budge an old pal who had been sleeping on the couch for weeks in the tiny apartment my friend shared with his girlfriend. Finally my friend announced he was going out of town on business, ruthlessly squashed the friend's hints he'd like to stay on with the girlfriend, packed a bag, and escorted the guest out the door. When the guest was on a bus out of town, my friend returned to his apartment, unpacked his suitcase, and resumed his life.

Bonus Tips: Sharing What You've Learned

Pass on what you've learned to incoming expats. When you've lived abroad for a while, you'll find that you have accumulated a wealth of useful knowledge about how to adapt, survive, and (with a little luck) thrive in your new environment. Be generous about sharing this information with others, especially new arrivals.

Pass on what you've learned to the world. When I started writing my travel and expat memoirs and my blog Enjoy Living Abroad, I realized just how much I had discovered about expat life, and I kept wishing that someone had told me this stuff when I was organizing my move overseas. Now that I'm a long-term resident of Spain who has visited more than 60 countries, I love passing along tips and suggestions to others, so they will have more and better tools for planning their own adventures. Many of the suggestions I post come from my readers, so if you don't want to start a blog of your own, feel free to jump in on mine to share your experiences, reflections, and advice.

PACK LIGHT

Quick & Easy Tips for Traveling Everywhere
with Just the Right Stuff

Pack Light: Quick and Easy Tips
for Traveling Everywhere with Exactly the Right Stuff

Copyright © 2014 by Karen McCann
First edition: 2014
Second edition: 2016
Third edition: 2018

Published by
Café Society Press
Hartland & Co.
1100 Superior Avenue East, Suite 700
Cleveland, OH 44114

Acclaim for Karen McCann's

PACK LIGHT

#1 Amazon Travel Bestseller

"Pack Light is a wonderfully concise and straightforward set of instructions for how to travel unencumbered, but still have everything you need. Look no further for the ABCs of how to shrug off that packing stress and enjoy your trip even more."
Ryan, *Jets Like Taxis*

"Karen's tips for packing light are bang-on. Packing light is incredibly liberating – give it a try!"
Nora Dunn, *The Professional Hobo*

"Karen, you are a suitcase superhero!"
Cat Gaa, *Sunshine & Siestas*

"I am a world traveler and thought I knew all there was to know about packing. Wrong! Karen McCann's tips added to my packing pleasure [and] will keep me focused for that next adventure!"
Nancy Todd, *The Spain Scoop*

"Her approach to packing involves common sense, and enough of the trademark Karen McCann humor to keep it interesting. I don't know if I'll ever have the courage to pack as lightly as she does, but I'm going to give it a whirl on my next trip."
Susanna Perkins, *Future Expats Forum*

"I know that both novice and veteran travelers will find this guide most helpful ... Karen has managed to pack a lot of good information into this small book!"
Jackie Smith, *TravelnWrite.com*

"Karen McCann has done it again, with another entertaining tome full of useful tips, gleaned from her years of travelling experiences with husband Rich. A genuinely seasoned intercontinental traveler, this expat expert recently survived a three-month trip with just one, yes one, small bag-on-wheels. To find out how she did it, rather than give away her secrets, I'll just recommend that you get the book yourself."
Fiona Flores Watson, *Scribbler in Seville*

LESS IS MORE

My husband — as he'll be the first to admit — has a serious luggage fetish. Over the years, our closets and attics have become jammed with suitcases, backpacks, daypacks, duffle bags, satchels, stuff sacks, roll-up bags, toiletry kits, and zippered pouches of every configuration. Paradoxically, Rich's goal is to travel with *less* baggage. We both love the greater freedom and mobility of packing light, taking only what's absolutely necessary in one small bag, even when we're heading out on journeys lasting several months.

For a long time, Rich dreamed of traveling like one of his sartorial heroes, Jack Reacher, Lee Childs' fictional protagonist who roams the world with no possessions, buying a fresh set of inexpensive clothing every few days and throwing away every stitch that he'd been wearing. I can't see embracing that as a lifestyle, but in a moment of insanity back in 2015, I agreed to try a six-day trip without any luggage at all, not even a purse. How did it go? Read all about it in the Luggage-Free Travel section below.

I was surprised by how much fun it was, and yes, we've done it again since then. But realistically, Rich and I agree that most journeys require more clothing, toiletries, and electronics than we can carry on our persons, even when we're wearing the kind of outerwear equipped with upwards of a dozen pockets. So we are continuing our quest for the lightest, most functional suitcases, seriously practical yet reasonably stylish travel wear, and ever more streamlined electronics.

Some people, of course, take the opposite approach. For instance, Paris Hilton once brought nineteen suitcases to southern Spain for a single month's visit. Even with a fawning entourage to do the heavy lifting, she described the unpacking as "brutal." The poor kid.

Those of us who haul around our own suitcases know that less luggage makes for more enjoyable journeys. Having just a single roll-aboard lets us step on and off planes without tedious waits at bag check areas, luggage carousels, and the offices processing loss and damage claims. We're less daunted by stairs, overhead luggage racks, and cab drivers who somehow fail to leap to our assistance. Airline bag-checking fees, no matter how astronomical, mean nothing to us. And unlike Paris Hilton, we never have to spend an entire, brutal day unpacking.

Reducing luggage to manageable proportions is one of a traveler's most useful skills. And yes, you *can* learn to do it. The trick is, of course, figuring out what you really need and skipping the rest. Stop groaning and rolling your eyes; it is possible — and this book will provide detailed guidelines that will make it easy (or at least *easier*) to identify excess baggage that you can jettison without qualm.

Having traveled to more than sixty countries, I've learned that it is possible to maintain comfort and style with minimal baggage — a philosophy somewhere between Paris Hilton's and Jack Reacher's, although leaning more in Jack's direction. Whether you're heading out for a weekend, a summer, or the rest of your life, you really *can* live well out of one small suitcase. *Pack Light* will show you the way.

In the pages ahead, you'll find references to useful websites and apps. Don't worry, these are not paid placements. I never receive fees for mentioning products and I don't accept sponsorship of any kind. Every link in this book (and in my other books, blog posts, and articles) is provided solely because I believe you might find it interesting and useful in planning your own adventures.

LUGGAGE

"You'll never meet a traveler who, after five trips, brags:
'Every year I pack heavier.'"
Rick Steves

Start with a single, lightweight, rolling suitcase. The bright red one I used for many years measured a modest 21 x 13 x 7.5 inches (54 x 34 x 19 cm) and weighed just 4 pounds (1.8 kilos) when empty. After long and reliable service, it started requiring duct tape on the bottom seams and kicked up a fuss whenever I tried to retract the handle; eventually, with great reluctance, I retired it.

That model was no longer being manufactured (possibly due to an excessive number of duct tape-related complaints) which meant Rich could happily engage in a quest for alternatives. After several months of diligent research, he selected the Biba Meri G semi-rigid suitcase in the small size, measuring a modest 19.6 x 15 x 8 inches (50 x 38 x 20 cm) and weighing 4.6 pounds (2.1 kilos). It has a nice configuration of exterior pockets for handy access to maps, umbrellas, and other necessities.

Although many vacationers are embracing the four-wheeled models, which are great in airports and on smooth pavement, I prefer the kind with two wheels, as they're easier to maneuver on rough surfaces.

Two small bags are better than a single oversized one. If you must travel with more than one suitcase, make sure each of them is small enough for you to manage on your own. These days you can't count on porters or bellhops being around when you need one, and the sight of a traveler overburdened with massive luggage inspires scam artists to offer the kind of "help" you don't need.

Resist the temptation to carry a heavy backpack or duffle. Unless you're a brawny nineteen-year-old or have the services of an entourage at your beck and call, shouldering weighty bags can cause considerable back strain. A backpack may project a romantic, youthful image; being crippled by lumbar and cervical pain does not. Be honest in assessing your ability to lug everything around strapped to your back for the duration of the trip.

You may want a small daypack or purse in addition to your roll-aboard. I use a light, roomy shoulder bag for holding water bottles, maps, and my sweater after the day warms up. I avoid carrying valuables in this kind of easy-to-snatch bag; we'll talk about better options later in the Clothes and Security sections.

CLOTHES

"Explore the world with an open mind, a sturdy carry-on,
and clothes that don't wrinkle."
Madeleine Albright

Adjust your fashion standards. Wearing multiple, subtly nuanced outfits every day simply isn't practical for a traveler. On the road, I'm willing to pair the same cardigan with every top and wear practical, neutral-colored shoes. My frilly silver sandals and hot pink sneakers simply have to remain in the closet for the duration. Of course, practicality doesn't mean letting yourself go completely. Living in Seville, I often see travelers trudging through the city dressed as if they were heading off on a safari or coming home from the gym. Dressing in an exotic, sloppy, or inappropriate manner tends to alarm the locals and make it harder for them to warm to you; it also shouts "tourist" and "rob me" to local thieves. You don't have to dress like a banker or a nun, but you may want to strive for a tidy and reasonably conventional look while in foreign lands. It can open doors and keep you safer.

Invest in easy-care, wrinkle-resistant, fast-drying travel garments. Leave behind must-iron cotton shirts and jeans that take a week to dry on the line. The travel wear industry is working diligently to invent ever-more stylish yet carefree clothing that doesn't wrinkle in your suitcase and, when hand washed, will dry overnight; TravelSmith is a great place to start. As for more intimate apparel, you've probably seen those ExOfficio ads with the slogan "17 countries … 6 weeks … One pair of award-winning underwear. (OK, maybe two)." I don't know who gives awards to underwear, but these have earned my vote. (For the record, they don't always dry completely overnight; if necessary, use the hotel's hair dryer to finish the process in the morning.)

Rich has narrowed his wardrobe to three essential items: the all-weather Koyono Black Coat Classic, which has 14 pockets (they call them "compartments") and a zip-out liner; Bluffworks Travel Pants, which have six pockets, three of which zip for extra security; and Jack Wolfskin Canyon Shirts.

For more on finding road-worthy garments, see the post "How to Choose Great Travel Clothes" on my blog Enjoy Living Abroad.

Buy neutral, mix-and-match clothing, with a few pops of color for fun. Life is a lot simpler when everything in your travel wardrobe goes with everything else. I usually begin with a jacket, a sweater and cardigan that can be layered, and trousers in black and neutrals. When I feel the need for some denim, I take my TrueSlim the only ones I've found that can dry overnight (although I generally allow two nights to be on the safe side). My shirts lean to black and earth tones, with one or two livelier colors in shades that don't tend to clash with one another when combined. Go as wild as you like on a scarf; if you tire of it, you can easily replace it along the way.

Dress in layers. If your trip will involve climate changes (and most do), pack clothes that can be worn separately or together, such as a tank top, long-sleeved t-shirt, sweater, cardigan, jacket, and scarf, so you can adapt easily to changing conditions. A warm scarf combined with slim wool gloves provides lots of added warmth while requiring only a modest amount of suitcase room.

Bring something to lounge around it. I pack a stretchy pair of trousers and a t-shirt that can be worn for relaxing in our lodgings, doing yoga, and sleeping; Rich favors a pair of loose cotton trousers. You'll be getting plenty of exercise, and your body will thank you for having something comfy to put on during down time.

Take only clothes and accessories you're prepared to part with. By the end of any journey, especially a long one, chances are some garments will have been lost, stolen, left behind, ruined by the hotel laundress, or given away in a moment of tipsy bonhomie; a few will have simply self-destructed under the strain of constant use. You'll be heartily sick of them all, so you're unlikely to regret the ones that fall by the wayside. In fact, you may find yourself depositing a few of your least favorite items in various clothing recycling bins along the way and doing the same with all the garments worn on the trip as soon as you get home.

This is why it's wise not to bring your most precious favorites on long journeys. When it comes to accessories, pack only costume jewelry that is lightweight, goes with everything, and doesn't represent a serious emotional or financial investment. If you wear earrings, choose the kind that snap shut or pack extra earring backs, which are easy to lose and hard to replace on the road.

Acquiring anything new means getting rid of something else. If you simply must have that amusing t-shirt or luscious sweater you see along the way, or if you identify serious gaps in your wardrobe due to unexpected weather or social situations, leave behind one or two lesser members of your collection to make room. Find a clothing recycling bin or place discards in the vicinity of public trash bins, where it's highly likely that someone on the street will be delighted to discover them and put them to good use.

FOOTWEAR

"The journey of a thousand miles begins with a single step."

Lao Tzu

Make sure you have a really, really comfortable pair of walking shoes. You're likely to be on your feet a *lot* more than usual. Rich calculated that during our first three-month train trip, we walked about five hundred miles. He favors the durable Keen walking shoes, while I find my feet are happier in sneakers. I have nomad friends who wouldn't dream of leaving home without waterproof or water resistant shoes to keep their feet dry on wet days. If your shoes aren't designed for wet weather, use a waterproofing spray to provide some protection.

Whatever footwear you choose, and most especially if that includes stiff hiking boots, buy them early and spend as long as possible — preferably months — breaking them in so that they are truly, deeply comfy. The last thing you want on your journey is fresh blisters daily.

Bring slippers. At the end of a long day of walking through the world, I like to idle around in soft footwear. I used to pack waterproof flip-flops as a hot-weather substitute for slippers; they have the added advantages of serving as beachwear and protecting my tootsies in any shower with questionable hygiene standards. However, I find that lately I'm rarely on beaches and never in dubious showers (thanks to better online intel these days) so unless it's killer hot out, I'm packing slippers rather than flip-flops.

Dressier shoes let you go out on the town. In social situations involving an upscale bar or a nice dinner out, you may want something a bit more elegant than everyday footwear. I often pack a slim pair of black flats that upgrade my look without taking up much room or adding significant weight to the suitcase. Rich considers his walking shoes acceptable anywhere. Very casual travelers may consider hiking boots fine for all occasions, while some women consider a pair of heels to be *de rigueur* on any journey.

Socks, like shoes, should be tested in advance. Make sure your primary walking socks are thick enough to be comfortable and don't take forever to dry. Bring a five-day supply, and when packing, consider rolling them up and tucking them into your shoes; you can wrap them in plastic bags first to keep them fresher if you wish.

TOILETRIES

"Live today like it's your last. But use hand sanitizer just in case it isn't."

Anonymous

Carry small, sample-size containers of all products and replenish as needed. You may not always be able to find your favorite brands, but even tiny villages generally have some sort of market or general store where you can restock, while urban areas offer a wide range of supplies at pharmacies, department stores, and discount chains.

If you can only find standard-sized containers, buy what you need, refill your travel bottles, and leave the remainder behind for the hotel staff or your Airbnb hosts. Refills aren't possible with some products, such as toothpaste or shaving cream, but when it's feasible, you'll save precious space and weight.

Keep all toiletries in one, multi-section kit. Buy one with enough pockets so you can keep everything organized by category: dental accoutrements, hair care, and so on. If you'll be flying, store a plastic, zip-lock bag containing all liquids in the roomiest center section. Keeping things in their assigned areas will save you countless hours of rummaging and replacing "lost" items that turn up later in unexpected places. Look for a kit with a hook so you can hang it up, saving precious space in smaller bathrooms.

Always carry tissues and moist towelettes or hand sanitizer. You can't count on high, or even basic, hygiene standards at every road stop, so you'll want your own supplies. I always carry a few packets of tissues and moist towelettes, and often a tiny bottle of hand sanitizer as well. So far I've always been able to restock these items along the way. Many stores also carry the kind of moist towelettes used to remove makeup, which is a great choice for travel. Not every brand is ideal for those (like me) with extremely sensitive skin, but if I have to use a less delicate product, I've found that simply running a damp washcloth or tissue over my face afterwards removes the irritating residue.

GOOD PACKING HABITS

"He who would travel happily must travel light."
Antoine de Saint-Exupéry

Remember the old golden rule of packing. "Lay out all your clothes and all your money, then take half the clothes and twice the money." Of course nowadays taking twice the money means making sure you have a debit or credit card and sufficient resources to cover any expenses incurred along the way. The part about half the clothes has never been truer.

Do a test pack. I usually gather my things gradually, well ahead of time. The day before departure, I make semi-final decisions and put everything in my suitcase to make sure it all fits. At this point I can still edit and adapt my wardrobe and dash to the store for any small items I may have overlooked. Now is the time to be ruthless about jettisoning unnecessary stuff — and to make sure you have included all the essentials. Consult the section Packing Checklists for Men and Women below while doing your finally tally.

Always arrange your things in the same order. This simple habit saves tons of re-packing and rummaging time. Although some people favor rolling everything or using packing cubes, I find those approaches add to the fuss without really saving significant space. I prefer to fold all my clothes flat and stack them on one side of my suitcase with current-weather clothes uppermost, then I set my little laptop on the very top of that pile. Because the laptop makes that side heavier, I place that stack on the bottommost side, next to the wheels, which maintains better balance and maneuverability. On the other side of the suitcase I place slippers and shoes (in cloth or plastic bags, with rolled socks stuffed inside), a small bag with electronic accessories, prescription pill bottles, and, tucked in the gaps, undergarments. My toiletry kit goes on top of all that. The suitcase's outer pockets contain things that might be needed quickly, such as a small umbrella, Kindle, and reading glasses.

Extra-Light Packing

"I haven't been everywhere yet, but it's on my list."
Susan Sontag

Experiment to find out how much you actually need on the road. Rich and I are constantly reconsidering our definition of what's absolutely essential and what can be safely left behind. We find that we pack about the same amount for a weekend, a three-month trip, or moving to a new country.

Carrying nothing beyond a few essentials, we're prepared to do laundry quite frequently. And if something wears out or we feel the need for a change, we can always pick up something new along the way and redistribute the garment we don't want via a recycling bin or leaving it in a public area where someone on the street is likely to put it to good use. Our style of packing is suitable for casual travel, when we're not going to weddings, giving lectures, or attending business meetings in corporate boardrooms.

And we keep tweaking our own checklists. In the run-up to our departure on a spontaneous trip that would take us through Spain, Italy, and Greece, with a day-trip to Albania, I decided to go even more minimalist than usual. (For trip details, see my blog post "Packing Extra Light for Our Most Unplanned, Disorganized Trip Ever.") Below is my extra-light packing list, with everything that I took for that month on the road.

My Extra-Light Packing List

Light jacket

17-pocket travel vest

Cashmere sweater and cardigan, black

Two pairs of trousers (black crepe slacks, fast-drying jeans)

Three shirts (two travel knits, one gauzy cotton)

Two long-sleeved T-shirts

One tank top

Yoga pants and short-sleeved t-shirt for lounging, yoga, sleeping

Socks and undergarments

Scarf

Gloves

One pair of shoes (comfy, supportive sneakers)

Slippers

Toiletries and medications

Reading glasses

Umbrella

MacBook Air, Kindle, iPhone

How did I refine this list from previous checklists? My long cardigan doubles as a bathrobe so I eliminated the robe I sometimes pack. The loose yoga pants I brought for lounging and beachwear were great for sleeping, allowing me to ditch the nightgown. And much as I would have enjoyed the option of a lightweight dress on hotter days, I knew I wouldn't wear one often enough to justify the suitcase space. I freed up even more space by leaving behind my hair dryer; I find our lodgings generally have one that I can use.

For a long time I traveled with three pairs of trousers, but I realized that if the ones I choose are really reliable — that is, they can be worn several times without bagging, will dry overnight, and of course, go with everything — then two pairs should be possible. And that proved to be the case.

Rich often travels with just one pair of seriously comfortable shoes, plus slippers for down time, and on our month-long trip, I decided to try it. I found that I loved the simplicity and comfort. Obviously this is not practical if you'll be going out for fancy meals, especially with well-dressed friends or colleagues, but in today's increasingly casual world, Rich and I feel more and more able to wear practical walking shoes just about everywhere. Having one pair of sneakers for a month worked out fine, but for trips lasting several months, I still think it's wise to take a pair of flats or espadrilles just for a change of pace.

Thanks to my iPhone, I no longer need a camera or all the attendant batteries, memory cards, recharger, etc. I still bring my Kindle and MacBook Air, although I've eliminated the need for hard drives, as I now back up my photos and documents on the Cloud and stream all our entertainment.

Rich's Extra-Light Packing List is virtually the same as mine, except he prefers his multi-pocket jacket to my light jacket and multi-pocket vest, and he always wears a hat: a Panama in summer and a fedora in cooler weather.

Not ready to embrace extra-light packing? Don't worry, I've got other packing recommendations you'll find more comfortable; see the section Packing Checklists for Men & Women.

LAUNDRY

After the Ecstasy, the Laundry
Jack Kornfield

Be prepared to do laundry constantly. On the road, Rich and I wash clothing a few times a week — basically any time we're staying more than two nights in one location.

When we rent Airbnb apartments, we always choose those with washing machines. If we're in a hotel, we wash our things in the sink; occasionally, I send out clothes to the hotel's laundry service or use a local laundromat, but often it's simpler (and cheaper) to do it ourselves.

Bring a laundry bag. A lightweight cloth bag with a drawstring comes in very handy for collecting dirty clothes awaiting wash day. If possible, buy one in a bright color that's harder to overlook in dark corners of closets when you're getting ready to leave your lodgings.

Use shampoo as body wash and laundry soap. This means you can carry one small bottle for all three purposes and save space in your toiletry kit. And you can get free replacements or top up your bottle at most hotels and other lodgings.

Take along a laundry line. While shower rods work fine when available, we find it's practical to bring a braided plastic laundry line. Sometimes we have to get creative about where we suspend it; a small balcony on a sunny day is perfect. You can drape stuff over the line, but you can also pinch a corner of each garment and work it into the weave, allowing many more clothes to fit in a small space. Pinching can leave temporary marks, so I dry my shirts on hangers from the closet.

Allow sufficient time for drying. Unless the weather is very hot, I usually do laundry only when I am spending at least two nights in the same place. Some garments can take even longer than that if the climate is particularly cold and wet or you're hanging the clothes in a very damp bathroom. If necessary, use a hair dryer to finish the drying process; you really don't want to transport (or wear) stuff that's still damp.

MEDICAL KIT

"Walking is man's best medicine."
Hippocrates

Pack your meds in more than one place. Divide your prescription medications and hard-to-obtain over-the-counter remedies, so that if one bag is lost or stolen, you won't lose your entire supply. I usually keep a short-term supply in my toiletry kit, some in the bottom of my suitcase, and the rest in the medical kit Rich carries in his roll-aboard. When it comes to essential prescriptions, I bring a bit extra, just to be on the safe side.

However, I try not to overpack, bearing in mind that when traveling through Europe, it's often possible to refill prescriptions at local pharmacies simply by showing an empty container or a photo of the prescription. That means I don't have to carry a lot of "just in case" medications with me.

Leave behind an extra set of vital medications that someone can send to you in an emergency. Especially on longer trips, it's comforting to know that a reliable friend or relative is standing by with a packet of replacement meds. If the medicines involved feel a bit personal, pre-wrap them in a sealed package, so all your friend has to do is address it and take it to the shipping service.

Carry copies of your prescriptions. Make paper copies or photograph them with your phone. If carrying paper copies, store them in a different bag than the medications, as you're most likely to need them if the bag with your medicine has been lost or stolen. If you don't have your prescription handy, copy or photograph the container, making sure the product name and dosage are legible; take multiple photos if necessary.

Assemble a medical kit. In choosing the kit's contents, consider your health history and that of any travel companions, as well as regional hazards and more mundane concerns such as blisters and upset tummies. Include a first-aid booklet and/or download a first aid app onto your smartphone.

If unanticipated needs arise on the road, consult a pharmacy. Your best bet is one near a train station, where they're used to dealing with foreigners and their travel problems; they may also be able to refer you to an English-speaking doctor nearby if the situation calls for one.

Should you have a more serious medical concern, contact your country's embassy or consulate and ask for their list of English-speaking doctors in the area.

Check out what other people take in their medical kits. There are thousands posted online for everything from short city vacations to journeys to the ends of the earth. During our first three-month train trip through Central and Eastern Europe, here's what Rich and I took along. In most cases, we just brought a small amount of each item, knowing we could go out and get more at a local pharmacy if necessary.

Our Full Medical Kit Checklist

Antibiotics
Cipro (oral, prescription)
Gold Bond antibiotic ointment

Heat & bugs
Insect repellant
After Bite: The Itch Eraser

GI woes
DigestivAid (herbal)
Citrucel
Ex-lax
Imodium

Pain, fever, colds
Thermometer
Echinacea
Paracetamol (acetaminophen)
Advil
Advil Congestion Relief

Cuts, wounds, blisters
Band-Aids
Nick Relief
Compeed protective strips (for blisters)
Butterfly closures
Omnistrips

Gauze

Adhesive tape

Sleep aids

Quietude (homeopathic)

Melatonin

Hangovers

Drink Ease (homeopathic)

Dental care

Poli-Grip (to secure any loose crowns)

Anti-Fungal

Tinactin

Allergies

Cetirizina Cinfa

Benadryl

Tools

Tweezers

Eyeglasses repair kit

Review and adapt your kit before every trip. On more exotic and remote journeys, we've carried a snakebite kit, a dental kit, an ace bandage, moleskin (although I now find Compeed strips offer vastly superior blister protection), and occasionally, in extreme situations, syringes. Fortunately, I've never needed to use one of the syringes we've packed, but I know people who have been faced with tough choices during disease outbreaks in exceedingly poor, isolated villages where everything, including syringes for urgently needed inoculations, had to be shared; it's just not a chance I'd want to take.

As it happens, our travels these days don't tend to place us in situations quite that exciting, so we are able to whittle the kit down considerably, with the knowledge that between Google translate and local pharmacies, we'll be able to supplement our medical kit's contents, buying whatever is needed at the time.

Electronic Devices and Apps

"The human spirit must prevail over technology."
Albert Einstein

Take a smartphone. This can provide you with a GPS, Internet access, your email, a camera, a flashlight, an alarm clock, railway timetables, maps, the total number of steps you've walked today, and oh yes, phone service. Many American phones are CDMA, which means the phone itself locks you into a local carrier. You want an unlocked GMS phone, so you can easily switch SIM cards, those tiny, removable chips that track your data and link you to a carrier. A factory unlocked phone costs more but gives you greater flexibility. If necessary, most phones can be unlocked for a fee either by your phone service provider at home or by an all-purpose, non-carrier phone store overseas. While traveling outside your own service area, you can usually buy a local phone SIM card at the airport or train station upon arrival; you'll need to change the SIM for each country. New travel SIM cards work in multiple countries with multiple providers, so you don't have to keep switching; this can be very handy if you're crossing a lot of borders.

Consider bringing a laptop or tablet. As a travel blogger, I spend a fair amount of time on the computer while I'm on the road, and my 11-inch MacBook Air gives me the full function of a laptop while weighing only 2.38 pounds (1.08 kg). The modest screen size is sufficient to enable us to watch movies together in the evenings.

Rich was an iPad man for years but eventually jettisoned his beloved tablet in favor of the slightly oversize iPhone 6+. The phone's larger screen makes it more comfortable for reading maps, checking railway timetables, and using all those other handy apps so dear to his heart. And it's small enough to carry around in his pocket at all times.

MiFi lets you use one SIM card to get Wi-Fi on multiple devices. It's a wireless router that acts as a mobile Wi-Fi hotspot. You just put a SIM card into the little MiFi apparatus, and it provides Wi-Fi cordlessly, via Bluetooth, to up to five different devices, such as your computer, smartphone, and tablet.

Consider bringing a travel recharger. This handy device enables you to recharge devices when you don't have access to an electrical outlet. We rarely use ours, but we always carry one on longer trips on the off chance that one of our devices might run out of juice at a critical moment. I'd hate to be stuck on a long train ride without a functioning Kindle or, even worse, a depleted iPhone, unable to check the railway timetable to see when and where I need to get off in order to make my connection. You top up the recharger again by plugging it next time you have access to an outlet.

Be sure to pack a universal plug adapter. I have a travel power strip with a universal plug adapter, which lets me use any kind of outlet to recharge my devices.

Bring a Kindle or other e-reader. E-readers are among the greatest travel inventions of all time, and if you like to read, you won't want to leave home without one. I used to pack five or ten books for long journeys and often ran out, at which point I'd find myself scrounging with an addict's desperation through hotel lobbies and second-hand bookstores for something — anything! — in English. Now I can download just about any book I want in ten seconds. If you're on a tight budget, there are plenty of free e-books available from your public library and other online resources.

Sign up for a VPN to stream movies and TV shows. You'll need down time occasionally, and kicking back with a movie or your favorite TV series is a great way to unwind. If you have an account with Netflix and/or Amazon Prime in the USA, regional coding blocks you from directly accessing your account from abroad. However, for a modest monthly fee, a Virtual Private Network (VPN) will convince your computer that you are in the USA, so you can stream as usual. At first I was convinced this had to be illegal, but everything I've Googled says VPNs are allowed in most countries and regions, including the Americas, Europe, Australia, Africa, and parts of Asia. If you don't have VPN, you can pay a fee to stream movies and TV shows from Amazon, or watch classic films, comedy news shows, and other free programming on YouTube.

Carry your own headsets. They let you amplify and improve your computer's sound and enable you to watch movies without annoying the neighbors on the other side of a thin wall — or the person sleeping next to you. To watch a movie together, you'll want two headsets and a splitter (a handy little cord that plugs into the headset port and divides to support two headsets). You may find your own headsets offer better sound quality and greater ear comfort than the ones provided on planes, making long flights a bit pleasanter.

Always keep your cords and small accessories in one pouch. With multiple devices, you'll want to be extra careful to keep track of all the bits and pieces. Mark each cord so you know what it goes to, roll it up, and secure it with a rubber band, twist tie, or lightweight plastic cord wrapper (there are various kinds on the market). Helpful hint: if you do lose a cord, check with the hotel desk. They often have vast collections of left-behind cords and other accessories, and you may be able to replace yours without spending a cent.

Download some travel apps. These can be phenomenally helpful on the road, and they'll be easier to navigate if you have time to play around with them before you go. Rich loves nothing better than checking out new toys for his iPhone, and in times of stress I often turn his thoughts to a more cheerful direction by saying, "Tell me more about that new app you found online…" After countless hours of investigation and experimentation, we've learned that those shown below are the ones we use most, along with a few emergency apps we find it comforting to have within easy reach, just in case.

For researching destinations, we love Triposo, which sifts through millions of websites to find background information on virtually every city and town on the planet. Occasionally we are thrilled to find ourselves in a spot so obscure even Triposo doesn't know its details — which we consider the modern equivalent of the spaces on ancient maps that used to be marked "here there be dragons."

For detailed railway timetables, we use the German app DB Navigator, which covers most of Europe. We look forward to the day we find ourselves going beyond DB Navigator on an extended train journey.

On longer adventures, we keep a few folks back home apprised of our whereabouts via a private link on Track My Tour. Rich uses his iPhone to mark our locations and add notes about where we're off to next; those entrusted with the link have sworn to keep an eye on our progress and, if we disappear, ride to the rescue. Or at least make a few phone calls on our behalf.

For other kinds of crises, we have !Emergency!_— which is the equivalent of an international 911 line. To cope at the scene, we have First Aid-American Red Cross and Google Translate, although it is my fervent hope that I never have to use both of these at the same time. I keep picturing myself attempting to apply a tourniquet while looking up the word "help" in Albanian. (For the record, it's *ndihmë*.) XE Currency will let us calculate the medical bills, and to keep in practice, we use it to figure out our bar tabs.

For finding hotels, we often turn to Booking.com, an Amsterdam-based company listing more than 28 million hotels, B&Bs, apartments, and other places to stay in 227 countries; each listing has an average review score to help with your choice.

For longer stays, we often turn to Airbnb, a peer-to-peer rental site that offers everything from a shared room (not that we'll be doing that!) to an entire apartment (our usual choice) to a castle (maybe someday). We occasionally stay at hostels, when we can find one that offers a private room with an en suite bathroom; we research them via HostelBookers and Hostelworld.

PAPER

"The most technologically efficient machine that man has ever invented is the book."

Northrop Frye

The single most useful item I carry is a small notebook. In it I write, in large, clear letters, the names and addresses of hotels I'm seeking, trains I'd like tickets for, foods I want to try, and a bit of local vocabulary. I have found showing these notes to people enables me to avoid getting bogged down in the quagmire of pronunciation or the futility of trying to get them to squint at tiny type on our phone screen. Hotel staff and fellow travelers often write things down for me as well, such as the name of the street with the taxi stand and how much we should pay the cab driver.

Yes, take a paper maps. Electronic maps are great, but when you want the big picture, it's still easier to spread a map out on a café table and spend time pouring over it, especially when you're making decisions with a companion. A map lets you see how things connect in all directions and helps you spot worthwhile detours that might otherwise be overlooked. I carry one map that shows our entire route (or, if we are traveling without an itinerary, the region) and usually pick up city maps as we go along. Often local maps come with a few handy travel phrases or information about must-see points of interest as well, and they let you circle destinations and scribble notes as you go.

SECURITY

"An ounce of prevention is worth a pound of cure."
Benjamin Franklin

Get locks and a cable for your suitcase. Ideally you want a small padlock with a number code you can set yourself; keys are too easily lost on the road. When you must leave luggage unattended, the cable will let you attach it to a radiator or other solid object. If traveling with a companion, you might find it more convenient to consolidate valuables, such as your electronics, in one suitcase and secure just the one bag. It's also a good idea to add zipper locks to your daypack or purse. These aren't actually locks but tough little clips that require enough tugging and fiddling to make it difficult for even the most expert pickpockets to get in without you noticing.

Consider clothes with hidden pockets. I have a 17-pocket vest that can conceal the entire contents of my purse — wallet, phone, Kindle, comb, tissues, a granola bar, and more — in its inner pockets, safely out of the reach of thieves. The manufacturer, Scottevest, managed to design the vest to maintain a smooth silhouette that does not suggest the presence of valuables, although fully packed it does make me look as if I've gained ten pounds. I generally carry only a slim wallet and my iPhone in the vest, nicely balanced in right and left inner pockets, and use my purse for less valuable, easily replaced objects such as maps and water bottles. Rich prefers a multi-pocket jacket which includes a compartment large enough for an iPad (and I don't mean a mini). He also wears trousers with eight cleverly concealed inner pockets. How cleverly concealed? Two months into our first long train trip, he discovered a pocket he didn't even know existed. These garments add a dash of mystery (I'm still trying to figure out the purpose of several peculiarly shaped compartments in my vest) and offer a safer alternative than carrying valuables in a purse or daypack that can be lost or stolen.

Find a configuration of wallets and document holders that works for you. Rich likes to divvy up his valuables and secure them in various hiding places in his clothing. His passport goes into the deepest of the zippered pockets of his trousers. Credit cards and larger amounts of cash go into a small document pouch looped over his belt and tucked invisibly inside his trousers. The belt itself contains a hidden, zippered compartment where he stores emergency cash and copies of our passports. Cash he'll need for the day and some form of identification go into an RFID-blocking wallet.

What's RFID? It stands for Radio Frequency Identification, intelligent bar codes (on credit cards, for instance) that emit information a tech-savvy thief could access. RFID-blocking wallets foil attempts to steal your information this way. I secure my money and valuables in an RFID-blocking wallet that goes into the deep inner recesses of my 17-pocket vest, and I put a little cash into one of the outer pockets for handy access.

Avoid waist bags and travel wallets on a neck string. Waist bags (aka bum bags or fanny packs) and wallets on a neck string worn under a t-shirt are obvious to thieves and positively scream "novice tourist with ripe pickings!" Waist bags in particular concentrate valuables in one tempting, easy-to-snatch package, especially when worn behind the back and out of sight. Our guide in Peru warned us about this — and immediately afterward his waist bag was stolen in a bar. (He knew the bar owner, offered a reward, and soon got it back.)

As for purses with cable-reinforced bandolero (across-the-chest) straps, they work well in those cities where thieves are cutting straps to snatch bags, and offer the convenience of keeping your hands free. However, they can put you at risk if someone comes by on a motorcycle and grabs your purse (which has happened to me twice). You want the strap to snap or the bag placed so you can shrug it off instantly. You really, really don't want to be dragged down the street at high speed (as happened to a friend of mine). No purse is worth that — especially one that, like mine, usually contains nothing but hand sanitizer, an old sweater, and the free map given away at the tourist office.

When you go out, fool thieves into thinking your room is occupied. Leave the TV on, with the volume just high enough to be heard through the door but not so loud that it draws unwanted attention from the neighbors or your host. For added protection, hang a "do not disturb" sign on the doorknob.

Packing Checklists
for Men And Women

Essentials and Luxuries

Every time we travel, Rich and I tweak the contents and arrangements of our suitcases. You'll want to create your own packing list based on such variables as weather, social settings, activities, and your personal preferences. If you're spending a week on the beach in Hawaii, a bathing suit isn't a luxury but a necessity; when you're wintering in Moscow, a hat and gloves are a must.

To help you get started, I've compiled general checklists of clothing and gear I consider essential for most trips, plus a few luxuries I like to include when I can afford the space. In the medical kit, I've suggested a few things you might want to ask your doctor to prescribe before you set off; if you'll be in exotic locales, be sure to check with a travel clinic about vaccinations, remedies to carry with you, and safety tips such as whether you should avoid drinking the water.

Whether you're heading out for a weekend, a summer, or indefinitely, the key to packing light is remembering that you don't have to cover every conceivable contingency. You can always buy things along the way, even in remarkably remote areas. In my experience, just about the time you're thinking that maybe you should have packed a sunhat, a local shopkeeper will be standing by smiling and holding out an armload of Panama hats for your consideration.

Even if I include a few luxury and optional items, when I follow the checklist below, the total weight of my suitcase is usually around 22 pounds (10 kilos), which is typically the limit airlines allow for cabin baggage.

Women's Packing Checklist

Clothing Essentials
Trousers; 2 or 3 pairs in wrinkle-resistant, fast-drying fabrics
Shirts; 5 to 7, including tanks, t-shirts, and long-sleeved tops
A sweater and cardigan that layer nicely
Travel vest with multiple interior pockets
Undergarments and socks for 5 days
Pajamas/loungewear
Jacket
Scarf

Clothing Luxuries
Dress
Skirt
Shorts
Bathing suit
Bathrobe
Hat
Gloves

Footwear Essentials

Sturdy walking shoes, sneakers, or boots

Bedroom slippers

Footwear Luxuries

Flats or heels for dressier occasions

Waterproof flip-flops

Sandals

Medical Kit

Any medicines you usually take (including all prescriptions)

A broad-spectrum oral antibiotic (prescription)

A broad-spectrum topical steroid (prescription)

Sleep aids

Pain reliever

Allergy medication

Nausea and diarrhea remedies

Cold medicine

Bandages

Contraceptives

Motion sickness remedy

Jet lag remedy

Insect repellant

Sunscreen

Toiletry Kit

Moist towelettes

Hand sanitizer

Tissues

Soap

Shampoo

Conditioner

Gel, mousse, hairspray

Comb, brush

Hair dryer

Toothbrush

Toothpaste

Floss

Lip balm

Moisturizer with sun protection

Cosmetics

Make-up remover cleansing towelettes

Nail clipper, file

Tweezers

Razor

Deodorant

Feminine hygiene products

Eye mask

Ear plugs

Sewing kit

Laundry

Laundry bag

Clothes line

Electronics

Mobile device (smartphone and/or tablet)

Laptop

Cords & chargers

Headphones (with splitter if traveling with a companion)

Optional Electronics

Camera, spare batteries, memory cards

Hard drive for backups and entertainment

Security

RFID- blocking wallet

Document pouch

Money belt

Metal cable and locks

Documents

Passport

Driver's license

International driver's license

Tickets

Car rental information

Health insurance

Trip insurance

Evacuation insurance

Vaccination card (if advised for your destination)

Copies of all prescriptions

Debit card

Credit card

Copies of all travel documents and cards

And Don't Forget
Notebook and pen

Maps

Eyeglasses (spares, reading, sun)

Eyeglass repair kit

Umbrella

Men's Packing Checklist

Clothing Essentials
Trousers; 2 pairs, with multiple hidden pockets.

Shirts; 2 fast-drying t-shirts, 3 fast-drying collared shirts

Sweater or fleece top

Underwear and socks for 5 days

Pajamas or sleep shorts

Loose cotton trousers for loungewear

Jacket with multiple interior pockets

Clothing Luxuries
Scarf

Shorts

Bathing suit

Hat

Gloves

Footwear Essentials
Sturdy walking shoes or boots

Bedroom slippers

Footwear Luxuries

Sneakers

Waterproof sandals

Medical Kit

Any medicines you usually take (including all prescriptions)

A broad-spectrum oral antibiotic (prescription)

A broad-spectrum topical steroid (prescription)

Sleep aids

Pain reliever

Allergy medication

Nausea and diarrhea remedies

Cold medicine

Bandages

Motion sickness remedy

Jet lag remedy

Insect repellant

Sunscreen

Toiletry Kit

Moist towelettes

Hand sanitizer

Tissues

Soap

Shampoo

Conditioner

Comb, brush

Toothbrush

Toothpaste

Floss

Lip balm

Nail clipper

Tweezers

Razor

Deodorant

Eye mask

Ear plugs

Sewing kit

Laundry

Laundry bag

Clothes line

Security

RFID- blocking wallet

Document pouch

Money belt

Metal cable and locks

Documents

Passport

Driver's license

International driver's license

Tickets

Car rental information

Health insurance

Trip insurance

Evacuation insurance

Vaccination card (if advised for your destination)

Debit card

Credit card

Copies of all travel documents and cards

And Don't Forget

Notebook and pen

Maps

Eyeglasses (spares, reading, sun)

Eyeglass repair kit

Umbrella

Trash bags to cover suitcases in rain

Swiss army knife with corkscrew

Duct tape (because hey, you never know…)

These last three items should probably be on the women's list too, but since I never bring them and Rich loves to take them along, they wound up exclusively on the men's list. Please feel free to pack trash bags, a Swiss army knife, and duct tape whatever your gender.

If everything on those long lists seems too much to organize, consider going on your next trip with no luggage at all. Madness? Sure. But it's good fun, too. See the next section, Luggage-Free Travel, for details.

LUGGAGE-FREE TRAVEL

The Seriously Minimalist Packing Option

I admit the idea seemed pretty strange — insane, even — the first time my husband brought it up twenty years ago.

"Why would we *ever* want to travel without luggage?" I asked. Until then, I'd always considered him a sane sort of fellow.

"Freedom," Rich said, growing a little starry-eyed. "Mobility. Imagine getting on a plane or train carrying nothing but a toothbrush and a passport!"

"That toothbrush isn't going to do you much good without toothpaste," I pointed out. From every standpoint — hygiene, comfort, fashion — the whole idea was ludicrous. And I said so, every time it came up, for the next two decades.

And yet one October morning I found myself — of my own free will — boarding a train from Spain to France with no luggage whatsoever, not even a purse or daypack, just a few small essentials tucked into my pockets. My resistance had crumbled several months earlier when I'd read about a travel experiment in which a woman spent three weeks on the road without a suitcase. "But she did take a purse to hold her electronics and toiletries and such," I said to Rich as I skimmed the article. That didn't sound nearly as radical as the nothing-but-a-toothbrush scenario. And then — I still don't know what came over me — I found myself blurting out, "OK. I'll do it. But only for a weekend!"

We soon hit upon a plan to take a train (our preferred form of travel) from our home in Seville to a French mountain village that interested us. As it turned out, exceedingly awkward transportation connections extended this weekend outing to a six-day trip. That's when I got serious about figuring out what I absolutely needed to survive on the road.

On the day of our departure, I walked out my front door dressed in durable, fast-drying garments and a 17-pocket vest stuffed with necessities: wallet, camera, Kindle with recharging cord and adapter plug, soap, deodorant, moisturizer, sunscreen, toothbrush, toothpaste, one of those little wire brushes for flossing my teeth, tissues, moist towelettes, prescription medicines, comb, mascara, lipstick, notebook, pen, and a sheet of French travel phrases. First on the list was *"Nous avons pas de bagages. Oui, je suis sérieux. Pourquoi? C'est compliqué."* (We have no luggage. Yes, I'm serious. Why? It's complicated.)

I had scoured the shops of Seville to find the tiniest tube of sunscreen, a child-size folding toothbrush, the flattest packet of moist towelettes. And still my vest was so bulky I was afraid I was going to be arrested on suspicion of being a suicide bomber. Instead, of course, everyone simply assumed I was rather stout. My outermost layer was a light jacket with big pockets into which I'd stuffed a silk scarf and two extra pairs of socks.

Rich's packing was far more minimalist, although he allowed himself the luxury of a full-sized iPad (which fit into the roomiest pocket of his travel jacket) for navigation and entertainment.

Our friends seemed deeply worried about the trip's hygiene challenges, but those were easily managed. We washed our underwear and my shirt every night in the bathroom sink; if they were still a trifle damp in the morning, we finished them off with the hair dryer. Other garments were laundered, but less frequently, or in the case of my socks and Rich's t-shirt, replaced along the way. All in all, we felt we maintained a reasonably civilized standard of cleanliness. We certainly never descended into the depths of squalor we'd known while camping in our younger days; compared to those experiences — a certain week in the Himalayas comes to mind — we were positively squeaking with cleanliness.

By the end of the trip, I freely admitted Rich was right: there *was* a kind of liberation in being freed from the fuss and bother of manhandling baggage. Every time we walked through a railway station or up a long hotel staircase, I felt a rush of delight that I was not one of the gasping travelers laboring mightily to haul around gargantuan suitcases. Getting around was simpler, easier and — I had to admit it — more fun. Why had we waited so long? As soon as we got back, I encouraged everyone to give it a go via my blog post "Luggage-Free Travel? Try it, You'll Like It" and my YouTube video "Forget Packing! Go Luggage Free."

Luggage-free travel isn't for everybody or, indeed, for every journey. Most of the time, I still prefer having more creature comforts and changes of clothing than I can stuff into my pockets. But Rich and I have repeated the experiment and found that yes, we thoroughly enjoyed venturing forth to see the world with the lighthearted ease of the unencumbered.

How To Pack Up An Entire House In 3½ Weeks

Yes, You Can!

When we moved to Seville "for a year," we never intended to make the transition permanent or to sell the Ohio country house we'd cherished for two decades. But as we gradually fell in love with our new life, we came to realize it was time to let go of the old one. And that meant selling the house.

Just two years earlier, such a decision would have been unthinkable. We had moved into that house as newlyweds, built a wonderful life there, and planned to leave it feet first in a pine box. We had lavished love and labor on the house and garden, built friendships in the neighborhood, and considered our home a fundamental part of who we were as individuals and as a couple. To walk away from it would mean walking away from a thousand cherished memories that made up our shared past.But the time had come to decide whether our future lay in Cleveland or in Seville.

Rich and I had settled into a new life we found fuller, richer, and more satisfying, a life that forced us to grow rather than making it all too easy to stagnate. The longer we lived in Seville, the less inclined we were to return to our old life.

Sitting in sunny sidewalk cafés all that spring, while Ohio hunkered down in the grip of snowstorms and bone-chilling cold, Rich and I spent hours discussing our options. We finally concluded that we weren't going back to live in the US at any time in the foreseeable future.

And if we were not going to live there, did it still make sense to spend the time, money, and mental effort it took to maintain an old country house and acres of property from thousands of miles away?

Since moving to Seville, we had gone back to Ohio only once, for a six-week visit the previous summer to make the necessary arrangements to extend our stay in Spain for a second year. While we were in Cleveland, I had found it difficult to motivate myself to spend countless hours repainting trim and weeding flower beds that I didn't expect to see again for a year. That part didn't faze Rich, who loves home improvement and gardening projects unreservedly, but back in Seville he used to lie awake nights worrying about burst pipes and squirrels nibbling away on our power lines (this had happened before and did not end well for either the power line or the squirrel). He pictured our pine trees catching on fire again, as they'd done twice due to electrical lines rubbing against the trunks, and he imagined tall oaks uprooting and falling over onto the house, as had happened to our next-door neighbors. He spent a lot of time exchanging emails with maintenance people, making sure the trees were trimmed of dead branches, the leaves were raked, the gutters cleaned, and mousetraps checked on a timely basis. Watching him fret about the house made me all the more certain we had to let go of it.

Although I knew all this in my heart of hearts, it took me a very, very long time to be able to say aloud, "We should sell the house." At first it felt like voicing the suggestion that I should amputate a part of my own body. It was worse than giving up my security blanket when I was four. But just like my beloved blanket, what was right for one phase of my life was now holding me back from the next. In a matter of weeks, the idea of selling went from unimaginable to a possibility to a probability to a certainty.

So now we were ready to sell, but would anyone be ready to buy? The real estate market had started going into serious freefall in the run-up to the global economic recession. Where desirable homes in our part of Ohio had once been snapped up in a matter of weeks, it was now taking a year or two and lots of price reductions to close a deal. We figured we would get it on the market in May and hope for a nibble by fall. We contacted a real estate agent who lived in our neighborhood and sat back to wait.

Four days after the house was listed, we had three firm offers at our full asking price. We went with the first offer, and over the next ten days our real estate agent negotiated the timing, inspections, financing, and all the other details with the prospective owners. One of the few real stumbling blocks was the schedule: the new owners were determined to be in by the end of July. Obviously this would be a tremendous inconvenience to us, but I wanted to do the deal and move on with our lives.

"But we're not going back to the States until mid-June," Rich objected sensibly. "Can we really clear out twenty years' worth of stuff in just five weeks?"

"Don't be silly. It's not five weeks, it's more like three and a half; don't forget, we have to drive to New Jersey for your brother's seventieth birthday party and fly back to California for my family's annual reunion."

Rich paled a little. "Can we do it in three and a half weeks?"

"Of course. I have a plan."

Scanned documents flew back and forth until at last the deal was nearly done. Late one night, the final sale agreement was signed and scanned and ready to go; all we had to do was click on "send" and the house would belong to the new owners. I noticed my hands were shaking. I was sure we were doing the right thing, really I was, but now that the decision was on the brink of becoming irrevocable, I felt a momentary stab of anxiety that was close to panic.

"Last chance to back out," said Rich. "You're still sure?"

I took a deep breath. "Absolutely. But wait one minute." I ran to the kitchen and poured two small shots of Rich's favorite Cuban rum over ice. I handed one to him, and we clinked glasses and each took a long swallow. "Okay," I said. "Let's do it." I moved the curser to hover over the email's "Send" button; we both put our fingers on the computer's trackpad and pressed down. The email was sent. The house was no longer ours.

Neither of us has ever regretted the decision. The timing, however, did complicate our lives considerably.

In June we flew back to Ohio and hit the ground running. I became ruthlessly organized, making a chart of the house and a plan for clearing out one room every day. Triage consisted of separating things into piles to pack, to set aside for the garage sale, and to toss in the trash. My sister Kate, who has moved a lot in her life, passed along one invaluable rule: if anyone in the family wants to keep an item, you keep it. No discussion. That saved hours, maybe days, of time right there. I borrowed some long tables from a neighbor and set them up the garage, so all garage sale items could be put directly in place. All items to be packed for storage were stacked in the middle of the cleared room. Extra trash pickup was arranged. It was all systems go.

We were up at six every morning, attacking the room of the day. We started with the attic over the garage where Rich had his office, and we soon agreed that many boxes of old records could and should be destroyed. At the time we didn't know of a shredding service, so we used our own home shredder, which soon broke down; we bought a second, which also collapsed under the strain. Finally we gave up and started burning the stuff in the fireplace, waiting until nightfall when the temperature would go down to eighty degrees.

"So this is hell," Rich remarked as we wiped the dripping sweat off our faces and tossed more folders onto the blaze.

In spare time that we didn't have, Rich and I made dozens of minor repairs to the house and grounds to comply with the terms of the sale agreement; visited our financial advisors, doctors, and dentists; and went out to dinners, lunches, and coffee with old friends.

At the time I didn't normally drink coffee, but I was starting every day with a Starbucks run and dozing off in front of the fire every night; it's a wonder I didn't fall in and burn to death.

Our neighbor Nancy, who was an expert in garage sales, came over to cast an appraising eye over the things we were getting ready to sell.

"Three days," she said. "Thursday, Friday, and Saturday."

"Not Sunday?"

"Never on Sunday; you just get lookers, nobody buys on Sundays."

Who knew? Our sale items soon overflowed the garage and filled the barn, the shed, and the screened porch as well. We put a notice in the paper and on Craigslist, and Nancy went out the morning of the sale to hang balloons and signs on the street corners. Some of the big items, such as the generator and the tractor, were sold ahead of time through newspaper ads, but the vast majority of the stuff was spread out for the world to pick over.

The garage sale was actually good fun. It was like a three-day neighborhood party where instead of a hostess gift, everyone brought us money and took away things we no longer wanted. The sheer volume of possessions we'd collected over the years had begun to feel overwhelming, a heavy burden we'd been carrying without even realizing it. Every item that departed was a small but heartfelt relief. We didn't really care when people pilfered things — mostly pocketknives that Rich had somehow accumulated over the years, which were set out in the one corner of the garage that was hard to surveil from the cash table on the driveway.

Almost without exception, our customers wandered onto the back deck and exclaimed, "My *God*, look at this *view*! How can you *stand* to leave it?" I felt a pang of regret every time someone said it, and Nancy, being a true friend, soon took care of this. The moment someone uttered the words, "My *God—*" she would ruthlessly interrupt and say, "But let me show you what's on the back porch," and drag them off to spend more money.

By Saturday afternoon we had sold an amazing amount of stuff, made thousands of dollars, and were more or less giving things away. On Sunday we invited back one of our Saturday customers, a Ukrainian woman with a large family and slender means, and told her to take any leftovers she wanted. Later that afternoon a friend's father arrived to collect the remains for charity. As his enormous boat of a Buick sailed away up the driveway, stuffed with the very last of the garage sale items, we were done.

On Monday professional movers arrived to pack up everything we were keeping. Rich and I spent the next three days following them around, relabeling the boxes. Left to their own devices, the crew had a tendency to write on every box "Contents: knick knacks," or as some of them liked to spell it, "nik nax." At the end of the third day, they loaded up everything on a truck and hauled it off to a storage unit until that far distant time when we would own real estate in the US again.

We spent the night at Nancy's, and the next day three Amish women — grandmother, mother, and daughter — arrived to give the house a final cleaning. They were incredible, especially the grandmother, who came up to my shoulder and leapt nimbly up and down stepladders wielding dust rags and soap buckets with wiry strength. By late afternoon they were gone, the house shining, clean, and empty.

I was alone in the house for the very last time, saying a private and tearful farewell; it is never easy to leave a place where you have been happy. And then Rich arrived to collect me, and we drove off, turning our thoughts resolutely away from the past to focus on our future as Sevillanos.

And in all the years since, we have never for one single moment regretted our decision to sell the house.

Note: Portions of this section first appeared in my book Dancing in the Fountain: How to Enjoy Living Abroad, *the story of our move from Cleveland to Seville.*

What We Took With Us When We Moved To Seville

Spoiler Alert: Not Very Much

Having emptied out the entire contents of a rambling country home with three bedrooms, two attics, a basement, a garage, a barn, and a gardening shed, what did we decide to take with us to Seville?

Three pieces of luggage and a rug.

We knew it would be insanely expensive to ship large furniture or massive quantities of household goods from Ohio to Spain. A little research showed it would be cheaper to buy new furnishings at the Ikea that had recently opened just outside of Seville. We decided it would be fun to start from scratch and buy on a shoestring, like newlyweds. So we took nothing but clothing essentials and a few precious reminders of home — mainly family photos, artwork that could be rolled and transported in tubes, and knickknacks we'd collected on our travels and now wrapped carefully in our sweaters for their next international journey. Two cheap, sturdy, hard-sided suitcases and an old duffle bag were enough to fit everything we wanted to take — except for the rug.

It was a gorgeous old rug, purchased on a long-ago trip to India and measuring a generous 9 x 12 feet in size — making it entirely too bulky to fit into any suitcase or duffle bag we could find. Eventually Rich came home triumphantly bearing a large, molded-plastic container contoured to fit a full set of golf clubs.

"The rug will never fit in that thing," I said.

"Sure it will," Rich said confidently.

In the end, both sides were proved right in the debate. Folded and rolled as tightly as possible, the rug could be squashed into the golf club carrier, but it was impossible close the lid; there was a gap of a good ten inches at the narrower end.

"This is a job for duct tape," Rich said.

For the next fifteen minutes, we wound duct tape over the gap and then up, down, and around the entire container to prevent it from springing open while being hauled about by the airline's baggage handlers. Examining the finished product, we decided the massive, misshapen lump we'd created might inspire security guards to check for the presence of a dead body, but on the positive side it would serve as a deterrent to thieves; no one would ever suspect such a hideous object of concealing anything valuable.

I did have one other serious concern: how would we ever fit this oversize piece of baggage into one of the compact Spanish cabs when we arrived in Seville? But by a piece of astonishing good fortune, the airline lost the rug in transit, found it, and delivered it to our apartment the following day.

"See?" said Rich. "No trouble at all, really."

And from that day on, I vowed to travel with nothing but carry-on luggage.

HOW TO MEET PEOPLE ON THE ROAD

A Guide to Forming Friendships
in Foreign Lands

How to Meet People on the Road:
A Guide to Forming Friendships in Foreign Lands

Published by
Café Society Press
Hartland & Co.
1100 Superior Avenue East, Suite 700
Cleveland, OH 44114

How to Meet
Locals, Expats & Fellow Travelers

The thing I love most about meeting people on the road is that they so often say things that I don't see coming — and then I'm reeling back in astonishment or falling over laughing, sometimes both at the same time.

Take Martin, our Airbnb host in Tallinn, Estonia, who moved there from England during the Soviet occupation. "I remember driving around with half a sheep in the back of the car," he told me. "Because in those days, when you went visiting, you always brought your own food."

It was Martin's Estonian wife, Erge, who delivered the real zinger. As we sat around their dinner table sampling lovely local wines, slim golden fish, blood sausage, potatoes, and various salads, she began describing Estonia's transition from the Soviet era to a free democracy. In case you're a trifle hazy about its precise location, Estonia is the northernmost of the Baltic States, south of Finland, just across the gulf, west of Russia, and north of Latvia. Its 1.3 million residents currently enjoy 100% literacy, universal free Wi-Fi, and substantial government support for startups, especially in the booming tech sector — which helped give us, among other things, Skype. I was deeply impressed by her nation's progress in the twenty-five years since the USSR pulled out.

Erge said, "We were lucky to have good leaders."

"Do you . . ." I had never asked this one before and could hardly get the words out of my mouth, the concept was so foreign to me. "Do you *trust* your political leaders?"

"Yes," she said, as if it was the most natural thing in the world. "I think they're moving in the right direction. They are honest. We don't have a lot of corruption."

I almost fell off my chair. No one had ever said *that* to me before.

This staggering statement piggybacked on another stunner I'd heard earlier that day. Standing with a tour group in front of the Parliament building, our guide had asked, "What don't you see here?" We'd all looked around blankly. "There are no gates, no guards. Sometimes when I am giving this tour we see the prime minister walking out of the building — alone. He just waves." She laughed at our expressions. "This is an open society."

Why We Feel
the Need to Connect

Spending time with people from a different culture teaches us how much we don't know about each other, how much interesting stuff has been going on, and how completely oblivious we've been about it.

"That's the glory of foreign travel, as far as I am concerned," says travel author Bill Bryson. "I can't think of anything that excites a greater sense of childlike wonder than to be in a country where you are ignorant of almost everything."

Swapping stories with chance-met strangers constantly makes us reevaluate our perceptions of the modern world. Until I went to Estonia, I would never have imagined that any twenty-first century head of state, let alone one living on Russia's doorstep, would feel safe walking through city streets all on his lonesome. This is just one of countless surprises I've had on the road, surprises that enrich my journeys and inspire me to make every effort to connect with locals wherever I go. Luckily, the people I meet think I'm exotic too, and many of them are curious about me and what's been happening in my corner of the universe, which leads to some interesting conversations.

As a travel writer, I'm often asked exactly how I manage to find all these opportunities to connect with locals in remote places.

The short answer is: by reaching out. The long answer — exactly how and when to do that — is laid out in this book.

If you plan to travel or live abroad, your online research will help you find ways to place yourself in situations that are likely to result in meeting interesting people, including locals, expats, and world travelers.

But before you start researching *how* to connect with people, it's wise to take a step back and decide whether you want to.

Not everyone feels it's a priority, or even desirable, and that's certainly a valid viewpoint. Some of my closest friends feel acutely uncomfortable at the very idea of hanging out with strangers. But if you're like me and find other people's lives fascinating, then you can use this book's simple guidelines for making connections happen. If you will be going abroad with one or more companions, be sure to discuss your social goals in advance to find out if you're on the same page. Many decisions, large and small, will affect how much interaction you're likely to have with the strangers around you, and you'll all be happier if everyone's preferences are taken into account from the outset.

One of the great things about online connectivity is that we can locate increasingly specialized offerings — such as a *Game of Thrones* tour of Dubrovnik, dinner at the home of a local chef in Athens, or an expat club for American women in Berlin — so you can plan activities that address your particular interests.

Have you always wanted to walk the ancient Spanish pilgrimage trail of the Camino of Santiago? Would you like to connect with an English-language book club in Rome? Are you crazy about rose gardens or World War II memorabilia or comparing the world's best chocolates? You'll find a host of apps and websites standing by with an astonishing range of information and opportunities.

About now you may be wondering whether connecting with people in foreign lands is really worth so much effort. I think it is. Not only can it make our time abroad more fun and interesting, and provide opportunities for our brains and psyches to stretch and grow, but it turns out that engaging with other people is the antidote to one of the most prevalent maladies of modern times: loneliness and feelings of isolation. These feelings can pervade daily life and multiply when we're strangers in a strange land.

LONELINESS IS HAZARDOUS TO OUR HEALTH

"The biggest disease today," **Mother Teresa** said, "is not leprosy or cancer or tuberculosis, but rather the feeling of being unwanted, uncared for, and deserted by everybody." In our increasingly mobile, fragmented, and isolated society, few of us enjoy the network of social support that our parents and grandparents took for granted. The number of Americans living alone rose from 5 percent in the 1920s to more than 25 percent today. And even if we are sharing living space with someone, that doesn't automatically guarantee a warm, cozy sense of belonging. In a study of older adults, 62.5 percent of those who reported feeling lonely were married and living with their spouse.

Being alone is not, of course, the same as loneliness. Many people, including an increasing number of older men, embrace their solitary state. "At this point in my life I wouldn't want to live with anybody," eighty-one-year-old **Stan Piotrowski** told the *Washington Post*. "I want to do what I want to do. If I want to sleep late, I can sleep late."

Stan Piotrowski isn't alone in this attitude. Many of us thoroughly enjoy solitude and use it to recharge our mental, emotional, and spiritual batteries, perhaps by connecting with nature or a Higher Power or simply luxuriating in a respite from the hubbub of modern life. But while solitude and introspection are natural and healthy — just ask the Buddhists — feeling completely disconnected from the world around us is not. It brings up our most primitive survival fears, the instincts that tell us being cut off from our community is tantamount to being left on a deserted hillside at the mercy of wolves.

Few of us have to worry about actual wolves these days, but there are still plenty of threats to our safety. Scientists have linked a lack of social connection to a wide range of health problems, including a weakened immune system, high blood pressure, insomnia, depression, strokes, and heart attacks. Loneliness takes a high toll on us.

According to advice columnist **Virginia Ironside**, loneliness is "a hunger — not just for human contact and companionship, but for a verification of your self-identity. The majority of letters I've had in my thirty-plus years as an agony aunt have been from lonely people — they don't have a partner or feel incredibly lonely within a relationship. Most of us feel lonely at one point or another. For some it's acute — a permanent feeling of isolation punctuated only occasionally by contact. For others, it pops in from time to time like an unwelcome guest, but goes after a brief visit."

Professor John Cacioppo, who pioneered the new field of social neuroscience, says that "chronic loneliness is harmful; but short-term loneliness can be positive and necessary because it highlights the need for social connections." When we feel lonely, it's nature's way of telling us something is missing in our lives and prodding us to take steps to remedy the situation. The professor's research suggests that seeing a therapist or other mental health professional may be helpful, but it can't resolve the problem, as it "doesn't fulfill that real need for a rich reciprocal bond."

Building a reciprocal bond begins with casual conversations that lead to deeper ones. When you travel or live abroad, you're constantly seeing new things and are likely to be surrounded by people who are eager to discuss them. Comparing notes with travelers, asking expats about their adopted city, or getting advice from locals on what to see and do in the region are all great conversational openings. These starter subjects can lead to deeper, richer conversations. For instance, discussing what you've just learned about a region's history paves the way to talking about how the city has changed during recent years, creating opportunities for other people to talk about things that have changed in their own lives. Now the conversation is getting real.

The Buddhists describe the antidote to loneliness as getting to know someone well enough to feel an active sense of empathy — what the 14th Dalai Lama calls "cherishing the well-being of others." Exchanging stories about yourselves can lead to feelings of empathy and bonding; this may last only as long as the conversation or become the springboard to an enduring relationship. Either way, such exchanges help fight feelings of loneliness and enrich our lives. Engaging with others in a foreign country can create many natural opportunities for this kind of conversation to arise — if that's what you're looking for.

WHAT DO YOU WANT TO GET OUT OF YOUR JOURNEY?

When we feel inspired to leave home and spend time in a foreign land, the first thing to ask ourselves is why.

What do we hope to get out of this expenditure of our time, energy, and money? This step can be crucial to enjoying and benefiting from the experience — and it's the one most people are inclined to skip.

There are plenty of reasons for going abroad, including taking a break from your career, spending time with family, or exploring a place that interests you. You might move overseas to pursue a job or educational opportunity, offer your children fresh horizons, or discover new ways to savor life. The list of goals is endless. If you're reading this book, then I'm guessing one of your goals includes meeting locals and engaging in meaningful conversation with them.

Interacting comfortably with strangers involves respecting each other's comfort zones. Some locals will be intimidated by your very foreignness. They may fear they can't keep up in a conversation about your home country, or they may not want to hear about your travels to exotic foreign destinations they can't even dream of visiting. I like talking about myself as much as anybody does (just ask any of my friends), but I make a real effort to hold back on that subject unless I'm sure someone genuinely wants to know more. When you stick to topics that enable others to shine, you can be pretty sure the conversation will interest them.

If you're traveling with companions, be aware of how comfortable they are chatting with strangers, and make an effort to create conversational opportunities they won't find overwhelming. You might be intrigued by the vegan food truck tour advertised on a hand-lettered notice in the vitamin store, but would such an offbeat option make your partner uncomfortable? Maybe you should consider a more mainstream alternative, such as a private food tour of the better restaurants serving famous local delicacies. You'll still get good food and opportunities for conversation, and your partner will be considerably more relaxed and happy.

Take time to consider your own parameters, too. The Internet is full of articles that suggest we are all seeking "connections with locals" and "authentic travel experiences," references that are often infused with the breathless reverence once reserved for mentions of the Holy Grail or achieving nirvana. But just how far out there do you actually want to go?

One friend met her limit in a Kenyan village, where she, Rich, and I had gone on behalf of a charitable organization that provided food for orphans. It had taken us days to get there, and all three of us were hot, tired, and a trifle preoccupied with our digestive systems, which had been sorely tried by various questionable meals along the way. One of the village's scrawny hens was sacrificed to make a stew, and when the cook dished up our portions, my friend looked down into her dinner bowl and discovered the whole head of the chicken staring back at her.

Without missing a beat, she said, "I couldn't possibly accept the head. You do me too much honor." And picking up the serving spoon, she returned the chicken head to the communal stew pot.

We all have limits and need to respect them. My friend drew the line at eating a chicken head and I don't blame her. Sometimes the real benefit of falling into an awkward situation is that it hones our ability to navigate life's tricky moments — sometimes with more courage, grace, and wit than we realized we possess.

Saying "Yes!" to Spontaneity

While engaging with another culture can place us in situations that involve small risks, usually there's nothing more at stake than a little social awkwardness or confusion. And the payoff can be a delightful adventure. For instance, there was the time in Bhutan when a small, impulsive act of courtesy led to an invitation to spend an afternoon with a monk in a remote Buddhist monastery. Rich and I were with a handful of companions hiking up a mountain trail in the Himalayas when we encountered a Buddhist monk and some young men carrying cloth-wrapped bundles and a few small pieces of furniture. After a brief conversation with them, our guide explained to us that the monk was climbing up to a monastery where he would spend the next eight years in silent meditation.

Rich reached down and picked up one of the monk's bundles, hoisted it onto his shoulder, and fell in with the men as they continued their ascent. This resulted in our little group being invited to accompany the monk on his journey. We wound our way up the mountain, into the monastery, and up endless, dizzying flights of increasingly narrow wooden stairs, until we found ourselves in the tiny attic room where this man would be spending the next eight years — 2,920 days! — in quiet contemplation, attended only by a villager bringing meals.

Someone asked the monk about his meditation practice. "In meditation," he said, "your attention is like the flame of a candle. It flickers and wavers, but eventually it always comes back to the center." He gave a slight wave of his hand to illustrate the point. "Sometimes it's like a fish on a line, it goes way, way out there." A more sweeping gesture. "But you just reel it back in. Every time."

Afterwards, one of my friends asked to have his picture taken with the monk, and that gave me the courage to ask for one too. He nodded and gestured for Rich and me to come sit on either side of him.

Now there's a delicate social etiquette surrounding Buddhist monks. Some have taken vows never to touch a woman, and even minor violations of this code require weeks of purification rituals. I certainly didn't want our new friend to be obliged to add that to his eight-year plan. So as I sat down, I took extraordinary pains to keep some space between us — no easy task in the cramped and crowded attic. And then, just as one of my companions snapped the picture, the monk reached out and grabbed me in a bear hug. I still have that picture, and the shocked surprise on my face, and the glee on the monk's, are priceless.

While spontaneity can lead to memorable moments, that doesn't mean abandoning all caution and common sense. At home or abroad, I wouldn't recommend going alone to a stranger's apartment for a look at his collection of KGB assault rifles or her tattoos of Hitler's greatest moments. But in most situations, you're seldom risking more than a little boredom, mild embarrassment, or that sinking feeling that comes when you realize they're serious about serving you the brains of the pig or a dish of fried flies. You can always say no; if necessary, you can always get up and leave.

Nomadic traveler Nora Dunn, who blogs as "The Professional Hobo," wrote, "On my first-ever overseas trip (to

China, when I was 18 years old), at a traditional Peking Duck dinner I was presented with fried scorpions. Being none too thrilled with scorpions while alive much less dead, I didn't try them, and have spent the last 20 years regretting that moment." To be honest, I would have passed up the scorpions too. But the great thing about having regrets like Nora's is that the next time somebody offers you an adventure, culinary or otherwise, you're highly motivated to take a chance and say "Yes!" to something completely new. And that's when things tend to get interesting.

Going Solo

If you've resisted heading overseas because you don't wish to go alone, you may be pleasantly surprised to hear that some people enjoy the way their solo status makes it easier to engage with others. "More than half of the time that I've been on the road since 2007, it has been as a solo traveler," says Nora. "I find solo travel to be incredibly empowering, and not nearly as lonely as I had feared it to be. In fact, it's actually easier to meet people and have meaningful cultural exchanges on the road as a solo traveler than as a couple or with a family!"

"People who have never traveled alone often describe their first solo trip as an almost religious experience," says a post on the *Independent Traveler* blog. "To take in new surroundings unfiltered by the prejudices, tastes, or preferences of a traveling companion can be heady stuff. Traveling alone gives you the chance to indulge yourself fully. Of course, single travel has its perils too — such as safety concerns, loneliness, and the dreaded single supplement. But a little preparation and common sense can save you money and get you through the rough spots."

One of those rough spots can be dining alone; casual cafés are fine, but in a nice restaurant, some travelers feel a bit self-conscious sitting by themselves. Rich and I often invite solitary diners to join us at our table, and we have been rewarded with remarkable tales of road adventures. One woman, an American textile trader in rural Japan, told us about the negotiations she'd just conducted over an elaborate dinner, with her Japanese clients attempting to discomfit her by presenting her with more and more outlandish and bizarre foods. "I am not a squeamish eater," she said with a grin, "and for a long time I ate whatever they put in front of me. Finally they brought out a bowl of broth with tiny live fish jumping in it. I did have to draw the line at that." Good call.

The most recent solo traveler we invited to dine with us was a British woman about my own age who was the only other person in the dining room of our hotel in Braşov, Transylvania. At our invitation she broke into a chuckle. "I got the same offer from another couple right here last night," she said. "When you travel alone people reach out to you in a way they never would if you were with someone." She joined us and regaled us with tales of her solitary railway journeys from her home in England to some of Europe's farther reaches. "I've never had a problem and I've never been worried," she said. "I like seeing the world on my own."

If you're considering a solo trip, for a vacation or perhaps to explore a city you might consider relocating to, the Internet is full of sites catering to the single traveler. Many offer a mix of practical tips and affirming philosophy. "Happiness can be elusive," says a post on the Solo Traveler blog. "The number of self-help books on the subject confirms this. Maybe we all need a little time to ourselves, to make decisions, discover our strengths, and experience more autonomy. Maybe we all need to travel solo."

Going solo doesn't mean being on your own all the time, or even most of the time. Tours — which come in an astonishing range these days — can be a great option, and many are geared specifically to singles. Google "solo travel" and you'll get millions of hits that include everything from hiking in Norway to boating through the Greek islands, to themes such as yoga, archeology, or "wine, food, and singing." Chances are there's a tour that will help you connect with like-minded people going someplace you would enjoy.

Finding a Travel Companion
(If You Want One)

If you dislike being stuck in a group but find the idea of setting out on a journey alone a bit too daunting, there are other ways to arrange for company on the road. Finding someone to travel with has never been easier; simply Google "find a travel companion" and you'll have nearly five million results at your fingertips. Finding the *right* travel companion? That's a bit trickier.

Much like an online dating service, some websites will, for a small fee, provide the profiles of strangers, which you can scroll through in hopes of finding a good match. I've never used one of these services, so as part of my research, I Googled one I'd heard of called TravBuddy and looked up their reviews on Lonely Planet's Thorn Tree forum.

"Yeah, I signed up and paid my ten bucks," a woman calling herself "seasickheather" wrote. "I was looking for trekking mates for Nepal and China/Tibet . . . my experience, as a woman, is that the only response/contact you get is from guys who are looking for a hook up."

To which a roguish-looking fellow calling himself "jjack" replied, "Pay me $10 and I'll meet up with you — cut out the middle man." Which I felt rather proved seasickheather's point.

If you are exploring this option, check reviews of the organization very carefully, and use even more due diligence when interviewing any prospective road buddies via email. Find out if their destination, goals, travel style, social interests, and finances are compatible with yours. Also try to determine, as delicately as possible, whether they're hoping for a "friends with benefits" relationship. If someone truly seems like a fit, meet for the first time in a public place so that if you sense something's off you can depart quickly and cleanly. While jjack is no doubt a great guy in many ways, I suspect five minutes in each other's company would be all we'd need to confirm that spending a month together trekking through Tibet would be a total nonstarter.

In the old British novels, such as *Rebecca* and various Agatha Christie mysteries, women who chose to go abroad would often simply hire a companion to go with them. I always thought this was rather sensible, if you could afford it, and so I was pleased to learn that a modern version of this practice now exists.

Flying Companions, for instance, provides a professional air travel escort to assist you in every way, from driving and hauling suitcases to sending your kids photos of all the fun you're having. It's not cheap; in a *New York Times* interview, filmmaker Janet Robertson said she paid $10,000 to send her eighty-seven-year-old Uncle Vin on a week's escorted vacation to London. Domestic trips within the US might run $2,800 to $4,500 and up. Uncle Vin reportedly had such a good time that he was already planning another trip with the same companion to Florida and had begun dropping hints that he wouldn't mind going Rome after that.

In the Agatha Christie mysteries, women who didn't want to spend money on a paid companion often recruited some impoverished distant cousin to accompany them, paying expenses but no salary in exchange for twenty-four-hour-a-day fetch-and-carry services. In many cases, the poor relative was treated so abominably that — well, I don't want to give anything away, but by the third chapter, tensions were rising, tempers were flaring, and mayhem was clearly on the horizon. This will, of course, come as no surprise to anyone who has vacationed with relatives. (Not mine, of course, but I've heard this about other people's families . . .)

TOURS

Organized tours make sense if you're heading somewhere that can kill you without even trying (like Antarctica, the Amazon, or Mars) or are notoriously tricky to navigate (such as Cuba or Russia). Most destinations are less fraught with difficulties and restrictions. Still, you might choose to visit them as part of a group for convenience, access to specific experiences, and the camaraderie that can, with luck, make the trip infinitely more entertaining. On a group tour, you'll have plenty of opportunity for bonding with a wide range of travel companions, possibly forging lasting friendships.

And there are more practical benefits. For instance, if you or your travel partner have significant physical limitations or health issues that could flare up during a trip, such as heart disease or bipolar disorder, it's comforting to know that someone will always be around to help you cope with an emergency. You want somebody to have your back if things go wrong.

Case Study: The Cuban Airport Crisis

I've been on several tours where things did go wrong, requiring creative problem solving and a quick course correction. In most cases, my guides rose magnificently to the occasion, but a few rapidly lost their cool and then their ability to function, allowing a bad situation to spiral into a total fiasco. I always assumed this was due to my penchant for independent, unconventional tour groups, and it would never happen if I went with a large, reputable organization. And then Rich and I went to Cuba.

If you've been in the Havana airport lately, you've no doubt heard the legend of the stranded tour group whose travel arrangements were fouled up so badly, over and over again, that they were forced to bed down for the night in a bus in the airport parking lot.

Yep, that was us.

Funny thing was, Rich and I joined the tour group because we thought it would *prevent* these kinds of ghastly snafus.

It all started when four good friends proposed that Rich and I join them on a trip to Cuba in February of 2016. That spring everyone was rushing to get to Cuba ahead of the American cruise ships and airlines, which were scheduled to start arriving in a matter of months, as soon as a few pesky international regulations were ironed out. Obtaining visas was a bit tricky (still is), and one of the easiest ways to get them was to be part of an "educational" group. So the six of us signed on for an eleven-day, twenty-two-person "learning adventure" from an organization founded in 1975, which has led 5,500 excursions to 150 countries, all geared to the over-fifty traveler.

As you have no doubt noticed, Rich and I favor independent travel, and we hadn't been on that kind of tour in many years, but we couldn't resist the invitation to see Cuba with our pals. As it turned out, we thoroughly enjoyed the company — not only of our friends, but of every one of the sixteen diverse strangers who made up the rest of the group. My sides ached every day from laughing.

And we had ample opportunity to spend time talking with all sorts of Cubans: artists, poets, farmers, fishermen, publishers, cooks, barbers, shop keepers, families running modest guest houses, and guys driving those fabulous old cars you see everywhere on the island. People were friendly and eager to talk, but at the same time guarded about what they revealed about themselves and disinclined to criticize anything about their country or government. Despite the dawning of an era of greater connection with the outside world, our new acquaintances were only too aware that in a communist dictatorship it is always wiser to show discretion.

This came home to us when, exhausted by the overly ambitious schedule that had us on the go day and night, we attempted to dodge a few activities, such as the 8:00 am talk on the history of music. This led to stern lectures about the fact we were there on an education visa, so failure to show up for even a single activity would spark harsh, if unspecified, retribution from the Marxist-Leninist Socialist Republic of Cuba. Yikes! By the end of the trip, even a simple walk through Havana felt like the Bataan death march.

The pace was a bit brutal, but overall, it was a fascinating visit and we had a grand time — until we went to the airport and attempted to leave the country. That's when our road trip turned into the existentialist drama *No Exit*.

At first we weren't too worried that our departure time shifted from early morning to 3:00 in the afternoon. Having surrendered our visas when we checked in at dawn, we couldn't leave the airport departure lounge, so we whiled away the day playing Cuban dominoes and eating Pringles from the duty-free shop. From time to time various officials would come over to talk with our group leader, but when we asked her if there was any news, she snapped and snarled and chased us off. Too overwhelmed to deal with us, she put her earbuds firmly in place and devoted her time to playing video games on her phone.

So we all took care of each other. People passed around cookies, produced domino sets, and shared advice for using the ladies' room (the locks were iffy, so it was wise to keep one foot on the door or take a companion along to stand guard). We checked in with those suffering from food poisoning and shared the one phone that was capable of sending a text message to the outside world. And to my astonishment (for I have seen plenty of people become deranged over far less trying circumstances) everyone remained remarkably calm and cheerful.

With enormous relief, we finally boarded our Aruba Air flight at 3:15. The plane then sat on the runway for an hour, and I sat contentedly reading my Kindle, listening with half an ear to the pilot's announcements that we were held up by an immigration issue. Imagine my surprise when that turned out to be us! Someone hadn't filed the proper paperwork, and we were hustled off the plane.

"This is humiliating," muttered one of my companions. "I feel like everyone thinks I'm a criminal."

"We are trying to arrange a rescue plane from Miami," the airport's travel services manager announced grandly. Rich turned to me and said, "There's no rescue plane." And of course, there wasn't.

Around 10:30 that night we were told they'd secured rooms for us at a downtown hotel, but when we arrived the hotel staff informed us they'd never heard of our alleged reservations and had no available rooms. No one did; at that time, Cuba was the hottest destination on the planet, and occupancy rates were close to 100 percent. My travel companions — or as I was now thinking of them, my fellow survivors — remained surprisingly upbeat as they took advantage of the opportunity to snatch a catnap on the hotel lobby's couches.

When our group leader announced that more rooms had been found for us at another hotel, no one even pretended to believe it. Still, we obediently gathered up our bags and staggered back onto the bus.

"We're the *Flying Dutchman*," I said to Rich. "The legendary ghost bus doomed to roam the earth forever . . ."

Our group leader spent most of the next two hours arguing with the bus driver in louder and louder tones until she was shouting furiously. That's when he stopped the bus in the middle of the highway.

"She's letting things escalate," Rich said.

"Never a good sign," I replied.

After ten minutes — during which, miraculously, no one rear-ended our vehicle — the driver put the bus in gear and started forward again. Our group leader had lapsed again into ear-bud enforced non-communication, so I went forward and asked the driver where we were headed now.

"*El aeropuerto*," he said. The airport. Interesting choice. And how long would that take? "*Una hora y media. Quizás dos horas.*" (One and a half, maybe two hours.)

Ten minutes later we pulled up in front of the airport, which was naturally locked up tight, as it was now 2:30 in the morning.

"Does any of this strike you as surreal?" I asked Rich. He just yawned.

Earlier our group leader had mentioned that we'd need approval for the cost of gas if we were going to spend the night on the bus with the air conditioning running. Apparently that approval wasn't forthcoming, because next thing I knew, the engine shut off. Instantly the crowded space became hot, damp, and fetid. Rich and I tiptoed outside, and so we missed the snoring, but I heard it was epic.

After a stroll around the parking lot to stretch our legs, Rich and I sat down on hard plastic seats bolted to a concrete slab near the airport's front door. I closed my eyes and took a deep breath of the balmy night air.

Into the velvety silence came the sound of soft laughter, and I opened one bleary eye to see a young couple with brooms, chattering and flirting as they swept the gutter, their voices rising and falling like music.

In its own way, it was an absolutely perfect moment. And I was reminded of why I travel — to feel pleasure in things I normally take for granted: fresh air, a bed for the night, some idea where I'm headed next. Would I have chosen to be there? No. Did somebody have a lot of 'splainin' to do? You bet. But the peace and sweetness of that night are as sharply etched in my memory as the wincing miseries of the day.

Not to keep you in suspense, we did get out of Cuba later that day, although they sent us to Tampa instead of Miami, where we'd originated. Afterwards, the tour company showered us with apologies, cash, and a discount on future trips with them (as if!). On our long, complicated journey home through various air transportation hubs, we kept running into people who'd just come from Havana.

"*You're* the ones who slept in the bus at the airport? We *heard* about you guys."

Yep, that was us.

I'll never sign up for another tour with that company, but our shared ordeal forged strong bonds among the members of our group. We still keep in touch by email when there's a story in the news about Cuba or stranded passengers, and Rich and I spend more time than ever with the four friends who went on that tour with us. Our night of homelessness brought us closer together than eleven days of good times.

Choosing a Congenial Destination

Whether you're going abroad for a brief vacation, a sabbatical year, or a long-term relocation, it pays to spend time choosing a destination that suits your particular tastes and interests. This may sound obvious, but you'd be surprised how often people show up to spend a month in a European city simply because they know someone who once had a dynamite weekend there; the fact their own preferences may be wildly different somehow never got factored in.

Rich and I tend to like midsized cities, with populations around three hundred thousand; Seville is about twice that size, but the old center where we live manages to preserve the feel of a smaller community. Midsize cities are large enough to offer plenty to see and do, but small enough to be navigated easily on foot. And there's a greater chance their citizens will be more relaxed and welcoming than those in crowded, ultra-popular tourist destinations. Being inundated with visitors may be good for the economy, but it can leave even the friendliest locals feeling cranky and jaded, with little time and less inclination to engage with you.

For us, researching destination cities usually starts with Triposo, an app that sifts through millions of websites to find background information about practically the entire planet. Occasionally — and this happened to us a few years ago in Sardinia — Rich and I have been thrilled to find ourselves in a place so obscure even Triposo didn't have any details about it. Rich and I used to refer to a really remote locale as being "out there," but now it's "going beyond Triposo."

Wikipedia provides a solid overview of almost any city or town. In addition to essential data (location, population, type of government, weather, and so on) it generally throws in descriptions of the city's history and economy, any UNESCO World Heritage Sites or other major points of interest in the region, and if you're lucky, oddball facts and anecdotes about esoteric saints, flamboyant rulers, and "famous" ice hockey players you've never heard of. It often concludes with valuable tips for getting in and out of town.

Wikitravel focuses less on background and more about what you're likely to experience. Some listings include detailed descriptions of various neighborhoods, helping you choose an agreeable area and avoid any with dubious reputations. If either Wikipedia or Wikitravel mentions local security issues, you're wise to pay close attention. Is this area famous for ingenious scams and tourist kidnappings? Then you might want to avoid it altogether, or at the very least be extremely cautious about talking to strangers while you're there. Your efforts to connect with locals can wait for less hazardous circumstances.

Getting Around

To me, one of the beauties of living in Europe is public transportation. Growing up in the car culture of California, in an area with very limited bus and train service, I bought into the belief that not only were cars the only practical way to get around, they represented a uniquely American style of independence. Driving long distances was practically patriotic. Now I find hopping on trains gives me much greater freedom and far less stress. While someone else fusses with the vehicle, I get to lounge about, drinking coffee, reading my Kindle, and making new friends.

I especially love the older, more traditional rail lines, still common in many parts of Europe, where you sit in compartments of eight seats arranged in two rows facing each other. This can create natural opportunities to strike up a conversation; an offer to help hoist luggage or adjust the window can be an ice breaker. Plenty of rail travelers are delighted to pass the time chatting, and if necessary will work hard to come up with enough English to make this happen. Asking a few questions about your mutual destination can spark all sorts of interesting discussions. We once whiled away hours during a train ride from the Netherlands into Germany chatting with our fellow passengers. By the time we arrived in Ostendorf, we had new insights into local political issues, the names of half-a-dozen must-see points of local interest, and directions to the best beer pub in town — in which we whiled away a very pleasant evening.

For European rail travel, Germany-based DB Navigator offers the most comprehensive railway timetables for just about any destination in Europe. In the continental USA, Amtrak is your most essential resource. The Man in Seat 61 offers terrific advice on train travel throughout the world. Want to have breakfast in London, lunch in Paris, and dinner in Milan? Thinking of traveling from Europe to China via the Silk Route? He's got it covered.

Any form of public transportation, such as bus or ferry, offers opportunities to encounter interesting people. Rich and I once arrived in Trieste, Italy by train and found ourselves unsure how to proceed from the station to the famous Tranvia Trieste-Opicina, an unusual hybrid of tramway and funicular that would take us down the hill into the city, enjoying spectacular views along the way — if we could find it. I spotted an Australian couple setting off, with an iPhone and an air of purpose, in what I suspected was the right direction, so I struck up a conversation with them. The four of us walked together for a quarter of an hour, then agreed that a restorative round of prosecco was in order, so we repaired to a nearby café. The conversation was such fun that when we eventually made our way to the *tranvia*, I sustained with equanimity the unwelcome news that it was not running at the moment and we'd have to take a plebian bus.

If you're looking for opportunities to meet people, cruise ships can offer you plenty of scope. Depending on the cruise line, you might not encounter very many locals, but the crowd could be an interesting international mix. The fixed price paid in advance keeps things simple and lets you enjoy communal meals and a wide range of activities with your fellow passengers. Among my friends, cruises are especially popular with multigenerational family groups. And they're a godsend for those with medical issues, mobility restrictions, or dietary needs that might make it difficult or dangerous to travel under less controlled conditions. To me, the sacrifice of flexibility and autonomy is a major stumbling block. But there are equally great advantages, including the luxury of not having to pack up and move on to new lodgings all the time.

Wish the trip never had to end? It doesn't! A converted ocean liner called *The World* lets you purchase a residence and remain in perpetual motion, visiting new, exotic destinations every few days. Prices run from around $1 million to $8 million, so start saving your pennies.

LIVING LIKE A LOCAL

Among the many reasons I won't be purchasing a home onboard *The World* is the fact that for me, the whole point of going abroad is to live among locals, in places that have retained their own character in the teeth of creeping globalization with its cookie-cutter conformity. In Seville, Rich and I live in an apartment in a repurposed two-hundred-year-old home that overlooks a crumbling church. Our neighbors are all Spanish, and I have learned to do things in the traditional manner, walking everywhere, buying my groceries daily, and drying laundry on the roof. Whenever I'm on the road, I seek out places to stay with the same kind of local flavor, whether that's an ultra-modern high-rise in Munich or an attic above an antique shop in Prague.

One of the easiest ways to find offbeat lodgings is with Airbnb, a company that facilitates private rentals of everything from a room in someone's home to an entire apartment (our usual choice) to houses and even castles. You meet the host to get the key, essential information about the place itself (tricks for using an old washing machine or a high-tech espresso maker, for instance), and suggestions for enjoying the surrounding neighborhood. Usually the relationship stops there, but occasionally it goes further. In Oxford our host grabbed an umbrella and walked with us through the rain to introduce us to his favorite pub. In Munich our host was out of town, and the friend who gave us the key proved so congenial that a few days later we met him and his mother for breakfast in a beer garden.

In Tallinn, Estonia, we were the first Airbnb guests Erge and Martin ever had. They really went the extra mile: picking us up at the ferry when we arrived, driving us to their charming rental apartment, and sharing stories along the way. When I mentioned my hair was in desperate need of attention, Erge called her own stylist, gave me a ride to the salon, and translated my preferences for cut and color.

When Erge and Martin generously invited us to dine with them in their home a few days later, we accepted with real pleasure. It was a delightful meal. We spent hours talking with them about life in Estonia and how it had changed after the Soviet occupation ended.

A few nights later, Rich and I invited them to dinner at an outdoor restaurant we knew they liked, after which we all went out for a decadent chocolate dessert. We wound up the evening at a funky, downscale bar, where they introduced us to shots of *millimallikas* ("jellyfish"), the bar's signature drink. Everyone in the tiny place offered sage advice ("Drink it down in one gulp," and "You'll want a beer chaser!") while a crusty-looking fellow in the corner played an accordion, and one of the patrons slid off his stool to do a little impromptu dance. After that, things got a little fuzzy...

Not all Airbnb experiences lead to sharing jellyfish at a funky bar, of course, but at the very least you'll usually have some interaction with a local at the beginning of your stay. Airbnb's free app offers navigational conveniences over the website and makes you a part of the online community. You and your hosts learn a little about each other in advance and post evaluations of one another afterwards. This goes a long way toward ensuring decent behavior on all sides. Be sure to study reviews carefully and read between the lines to discover what isn't being said. Faint praise should be considered a possible red flag.

Airbnb Experiences is a new part of the service. It includes a wide variety of entertainment, tours, food tastings, classes, and just about anything else you can imagine and then some. If you've ever wanted to connect with your inner street artist, sushi chef, or surfer, now's your chance to do it — in a place where nobody knows the everyday you. And while you're at it, you'll be connecting with locals, expats, and fellow travelers under circumstances that will give you all plenty to talk about.

If you happen to be over fifty, there's a new option that young journalists like to refer to as "Airbnb for seniors." The Freebird Club brings together hosts and guests in that age group who want companionship and conversation to be part of the package. You not only stay in the hosts' home but are invited to engage socially with them. The 2015 start-up was tested on a small scale in Ireland and the UK, and it's now serving twenty-three countries.

Freebird Club founder Peter Mangan got the idea when he started renting his home to travelers and asked his father to meet guests and give them the key. "There was just a natural bonding," he recalls. "Before you knew it, they were down at the pub on a Tuesday evening. He'd be telling them about nice places to go, and he might take them there, and they'd invite him back to the house for dinner. It was all happening very naturally." I haven't had the opportunity to try this lodging club myself, but I have to say that does sound like more fun than sitting alone in your hotel room.

Another alternative to staying in hotels is the more sociable environment of a hostel. They're definitely not just for young people anymore; while kids make up the majority in some, you'll often find people of all ages, including business travelers, retirees, and family groups. Low prices, the availability of a kitchen, and common areas where you can hang out and chat with fellow travelers from around the world make for an attractive package. I'm not big on dormitories, but luckily for me many hostels now offer private rooms for couples, often with a private bathroom.

Rich and I stayed at a great hostel in the mountain town of Veliko Tarnovo, Bulgaria's former capital. We paid twenty-eight dollars a night for a private bedroom with its own *en suite* bathroom. Of course, we had to forego hotel luxuries such as chocolates on our pillows, concierge services, and heat anywhere outside the public gathering areas; it was autumn, and our private room felt like a meat locker at night. But the dining hall was toasty warm all day, and over breakfast and dinner we spent many happy hours in conversation with interesting folks from a dozen countries. Sites such as HostelBookers and Hostelworld are filled with listings; be sure to check reviews carefully to determine if the hostel meets your standards, appeals to a crowd that sounds interesting to you, and offers a kitchen or other communal space for social interaction.

BREAKING BREAD TOGETHER

Sharing a meal is a great way to get to know people, and a whole new industry has sprung up to provide private dining experiences. This is a boon to both travelers and people relocating to a city, as the leisurely pace of the meal provides plenty of opportunities to bring up subjects you're curious about and discover what your hosts and your fellow diners have to say about the culture, community, and region.

Booking through one of the best-known private-meal companies, EatWith, Rich and I have enjoyed memorable dinners in California, Spain, Croatia, Lithuania, and Greece. Often called "the Airbnb of dining," EatWith enables you to connect with a local chef who is offering a private dinner, usually in his or her home. You can check out menus, reviews, costs, whether wine is included, and if there's room for you at the table. The number of guests is usually eight to twelve, depending on the size of the host's dinner table; occasionally meals are held in larger venues, such as EatWith's headquarters in San Francisco or the cooking school in Seville's Triana Market. The cost is about what you'd spend at a good local restaurant. As with Airbnb, you book online, pay in advance, and never have to worry about currency conversion, cash tips, or hidden extras.

The best EatWith dinner we've ever had was prepared by a dentist named Lidija, who had just qualified as the organization's first host in Zagreb, Croatia. Joining us at the table were her daughter Doris and longtime friend Mladen, who immediately produced a test tube of orange *rakija* (fruit brandy) and invited us to try it. From that first moment, the evening flowed forward, the conversation rolling around the table as easily as if we were old friends.

Dinner was served on Lidija's balcony to take advantage of the unseasonable warm weather, known locally, Mladen explained, as "old woman summer." We began with *viška pogača*, bread topped with olive oil, onions, and anchovies.

"The recipe comes from the island of Vis, in southern Croatia," said Lidija. "Traditionally it is made with a second crust on top, but that is too much bread, I think."

A summer salad of tomato, cheese, and olives followed, and then Lidija brought out the main course: fresh *skuša riba* (mackerel) cooked to perfection, dense yet flaky, surrounded with organic potatoes. The side dish was *blitva*, a vegetable nobody knew how to translate.

"It's like kale, but it's not," said Doris.

One of the things I loved best about this dinner was that nobody reached for a smartphone to look up the translation; we were having way too much fun to bother with technical details like that. (For the record, I later discovered that *blitva* is a Dalmatian relative of Swiss chard.)

Dessert was *rožata*—a cross between flan and *crème brûlée*, topped with sour cherries soaked in *rakija* — accompanied by small, sweet purple grapes from Lidija's garden. We all had so much fun that we met again for drinks on our last night in town. Six months later Doris came to visit us in Seville, and we had the pleasure of introducing her to the Feria de Abril (April Fair); there's talk of all of us getting together again either in Croatia or Spain.

EatWith is available in many countries, but if there isn't one scheduled for a place and time that works for you, try one of the others, such as Eat with a Local or Traveling Spoon; many of their chefs incorporate cooking classes into the experience. Or Google "pop-up dinner" plus the name of the city. Pop-ups are one-night-only meals provided by local chefs looking to build a reputation and clientele, and the food and conversation are likely to be stellar. Pop-ups may be held in a chef's home or in a larger or more offbeat venue; the last one we went to was held in what appeared to be a yoga studio in San Francisco.

The yoga studio dinner was arranged by Feastly, which originated in the US but is now branching out around the world. "The dinner table is the original social network," founder Noah Karesh told the *New York Times*, and meals offer "the easiest and best way to understand and interact with new cultures." He's so right; sharing a meal gives everyone plenty of time to get to know each other in a relaxed setting, with the shared experience of new foods to enliven the conversation. If your goal is to do a bit of research on a town you're considering moving to, there's no better place to start than a communal meal in a local home.

When private dining options are not available, Rich and I often sign up for culinary tours, which tend to be quirky, individualistic adventures that are as much about savoring the local culture as regional delicacies. Groups are small; we sometimes find it's just us, and at most there will be a handful of others from various countries. Formats vary widely, but typically these are walking tours lasting several hours, during which you visit markets, bakeries, delicatessens, street carts, and restaurants in the company of a knowledgeable and engaging guide. Often there are opportunities for you to chat with chefs, bakers, brewers, and families running traditional food stalls in the farmers' market.

My first such tour was Chris Milano's Foodie Adventures, which took us to San Francisco's Chinatown and neighboring North Beach, the Italian section of town. Having grown up in the Bay Area, I'm no stranger to the city, but Chris's tour was full of surprises. We ate amazing dim sum from a back-alley hole-in-the-wall, met a grandfather who writes fortunes for Chinese fortune cookies (including the racy ones designed for bachelor parties), and threaded our way through labyrinthine shops selling alligator legs and live turtles which must, according to hand-lettered signs, be killed before you take them off the premises. Fresh focaccia bread, homemade salami, and pork melting off the bone were served in some of the few places in North Beach that are still run by Italians; Chinatown is quickly swallowing up the old European section. Chris had plenty to say about the city, how it is changing, and how the increasing diversity means both heartbreaking losses and fabulous new choices about what to eat for lunch.

Sometimes food tour conversations lead to further encounters that can blossom into friendships. During a recent trip to Athens, Rich and I joined a guide and two other couples for a stroll around the city center, where we sampled honey and yogurt, enjoyed the catch of the day fried up with lemons at a café in the fish market, and sipped coffee brewed in an *ibrik* pot set in hot sand. We had such fun swapping cooking stories with one couple that we met up at a restaurant two nights later, then organized another rendezvous at a dinner we'd arranged in the home of a local chef we'd found via EatWith. On our last day in town Rich and I took a long walk to a bohemian restaurant we'd read about on the other side of the city — and there sat this couple having lunch. It's pretty clear that fate has some sort of plan in mind for the four of us; when I figure out what it is, I'll let you know. Whatever it turns out to be, you can be sure it will include some seriously delicious food.

There's no central food tour registry, so you'll have to Google your destination city and add "food tour" or "culinary tour." If you happen to be in Spain, my friend Lauren runs Devour Tours, which provides terrific food and culture tours in six cities, including Seville. Major metropolitan centers like Paris will give you a vast array of options; in more obscure cities and some large towns you might find one or two. Some have themes, such as regional delicacies or food and wine pairings. All will provide opportunities for discussing the local cuisine with people who know a lot about the area, the best places to eat, and local delicacies that are simply too good to miss.

LET'S MEET OVER DRINKS

As you may have observed, adult beverages have a tendency to foster rapid bonhomie in any country. One night on a road trip, Rich and I wandered into Kewl Cats, a karaoke bar in Merced, an agricultural town in California's Central Valley. When we learned that the weekly trivia contest was about to start, we instantly signed up. The other players could not have been friendlier — or more compassionate about our pathetic scores. By the end of the evening, everyone was urging us to come back the following week, and I sincerely wished that we could. As long as we managed to avoid getting drawn into actual karaoke — our lack of talent at trivia is nothing compared to our inability to sing — it was my kind of bar.

Finding the Kewl Cats was sheer luck; it just happened to be the closest tavern to our hotel. But if you're interested in raising a glass with friendly strangers, there are pub crawls and wine tastings on offer in many cities. Like food tours, these tend to be quirky, one-of-a-kind, private ventures, and there's no central website for them. But if you Google your destination city and add the type of tour you'd like, chances are you'll find plenty to choose from. Read the descriptions carefully; an expensive wine lover's gathering in a chateau outside of Paris will draw a very different crowd than the Warsaw pub crawl that includes free shots, drinking games, and late-night clubbing.

One great way to meet people over drinks is InterNations, the expat social network that holds casual gatherings in 420 cities around the world. Rich and I are longtime members of the Seville branch and sign up to attend in other cities that we happen to be passing through. Most gatherings are simply meetups in bars, where you pay for your own drinks and wander about striking up conversations; since everyone else is there for the same purpose, it's easy to find people who are happy to chat with you and fill you in on the local scene. Larger chapters have subsections that organize dinners, cultural activities, and theme parties.

When we show up at an InterNations gathering anywhere in the world, we expect welcoming smiles, a sticker printed with our name and nationality, and a room full of interesting locals and expats. Only once, at an InterNations gathering at an upscale hotel in Stockholm, did we get a very different reception.

There were no greeters waiting as we stepped out onto the designated balcony, so we made our way to the bar, ordered a couple of beers, and turned to survey the crowd. We found ourselves surrounded by beautifully groomed young men and women who were talking, laughing, and — as soon as they noticed us — glaring in our direction before pointedly turning their backs. Clearly our very presence was sucking all the trendiness out of the occasion. I felt a powerful urge to drop to my belly and crawl to the elevator.

"We have to get out of here!" I hissed to Rich.

"As fast as possible," he agreed and began chugging his Heineken.

"Leave it," I urged.

"Are you kidding? These beers cost nine dollars apiece!"

It didn't take long to work out what had happened. In our excitement at discovering that an InterNations event coincided with our visit to Stockholm, we had overlooked one teeny, tiny detail: this was not an event for the main group but a young singles night. *Hoppsan!* (That's Swedish for "Oops!") Rich and I guzzled our drinks and fled. I swear I heard a collective sigh of relief as we passed through the exit doors.

Aside from that mortifying faux pas, InterNations has been a great way for us to meet people. Normally an InterNations gathering includes locals as well as expats from a dozen countries, and the age range can span six decades. Some chapters attract a lot of younger business people, who exchange cards and flirt madly with one another; others draw an older crowd of folks who bring a lot of experience to the art of telling travel stories. In Europe there is far less of a generational divide than in the States; we've struck up conversations with people twenty or thirty years our juniors who emailed the next day to invite us out for drinks or dinner. One of the great things about being older is that we don't worry about such invitations leading to romantic misunderstandings or unwelcome sexual advances; younger or single travelers will obviously want to use their common sense about this. But in general, InterNations provides a comfortable way to meet a great many people over drinks in a casual setting, and this is a tremendous boon to travelers and to people living abroad.

Sightseeing

When you find yourself in an unfamiliar place, one of the best ways to get your bearings is to take a walking tour. During one of our early visits to Seville, somewhere around 2002, we couldn't find an official tour anywhere, but eventually noticed a tattered flier on a phone booth offering "The Carmen Tour of Seville" in English every evening. When we showed up for it, we met Johanna, a vivacious young Belgian woman who gave us a condensed version of the opera Carmen using puppets, accordion, and song, interspersed with running commentary about Seville's legends and history as we strolled through the streets.

It was a marvelous tour, and we not only learned a lot about the city that was to become our home, but Johanna became one of our first friends there. One night in a tapas bar she told us about her first serious faux pas in Spanish. "I got to know some of the gypsies who give carriage rides around the cathedral," she said. " One of them had rounder features rather than the more common high cheekbones. I was trying to say, 'but you don't have gypsy *huesos* (bones),' but instead I said, 'you don't have gypsy *huevos*' — which as you probably know means eggs, but is a slang term for testicles. I couldn't understand why all his friends were laughing so hysterically."

Johanna didn't charge a set fee for "Carmen." In the manner of most free walking tours, when it was over she set out a bag and invited people to donate what they wished. If I'm in a strange town and find there's a free walking tour, I usually take it — not to avoid paying (I often give as much as a standard tour would run) but because these tours tend to be livelier. The guides work extra hard to be entertaining in order to earn tips and to encourage you to sign up for additional paid tours. As you walk around together, the flow of interesting historical tidbits and jokes make it easy to exchange a few remarks with others in the group. At the conclusion of the formal tour, the group is often invited into some sort of pub, letting the social interaction blossom over beer and lunch. If not, Rich and I sometimes get to know fellow participants well enough that we feel comfortable suggesting we all grab a bite together afterwards.

Many excellent tours are not affiliated with any larger group, but one that we've found reliable is Sandeman's New Europe Tours, which operates both free and paid walking tours in eighteen cities. They recently began operating in Seville, but when people ask me for a referral, I always send them to Spain Savvy my friend Sarah's outstanding boutique tour company, where I know they'll get individual attention and see *Sevilla profunda* (the real Seville).

If you're footsore from long days of touring and want to see the sights in motorized comfort, there are many options, starting with the ubiquitous Hop-On, Hop-Off bus tours. In addition to providing cultural commentary, it's a handy form of transportation that lets you visit the top attractions and earmark areas to explore on your own later. The quality of the commentary varies widely. A woman I met at a language school told me that she was part of an EU program that paid for her to travel from the UK to Seville, take a month of lessons, then work for a month to practice Spanish on the job. She was placed on one of Seville's Hop-On, Hop-Off buses and handed a microphone. "It was a disaster," she told me ruefully. "I could barely read the notes they gave me. Finally one of the Spanish passengers jumped up and took the microphone away from me and read the stuff himself." She shuddered. "I can't wait until my month is over." I'm sure she wasn't alone in that sentiment.

As a travel writer, I occasionally convince Rich that we should sign up for some cheesy tour that might be fun to blog about. That's how we wound up on Warsaw's "3-hour Communist Tour in an Original Socialist Van" led by a young man named Lucas. Like just about everything we encountered in the Polish capital, this activity didn't turn out as expected. It was meant to be a small, English-language tour, yet somehow it included an entire Lithuanian bachelor party that hadn't slept in days, four Spaniards who spoke almost no English, and three others besides ourselves who actually listened to Lucas' spiel.

We drove around town for hours in two noisy, sweltering Soviet-era vans. The Lithuanians kept darting into shops to buy more liters of beer and finally disappeared altogether somewhere around the old headquarters of the Central Committee of the Polish United Worker's Party. The rest of us went on to the underwhelming Museum of Life Under Communism, where in a kitchen that was meant to recreate the feel of 1970s Warsaw, we were given shots of cheap, mint-flavored and cherry-flavored vodka. We were supposed to view some 1950s propaganda films and sample the traditional, down-and-dirty snack of bread with pork lard and pickles, but none of that ever materialized. And perhaps that's just as well.

Were Rich and I sorry we'd signed up for the less-than-stellar "3-Hour Communism Tour in an Original Socialist Van"? Not at all. Because we've learned that bad times make the best stories. Nobody wants to hear about the connections we make with ample time, the flawless white sand beaches we stroll upon, or the bartenders who really know how to fashion a dry martini. As delightful as such experiences are when they happen to me, I find telling those stories to others tends to elicit yawns and snores. But we all love listening to tales of disasters averted and challenges overcome. When I tell stories about Warsaw, people are far more interested in the Lithuanian bachelor party and pork lard snacks than the charming Airbnb apartment we rented in that city.

Lucas knew all about the spellbinding effect of describing misadventures, and he held the English-speaking members of our group riveted with a story that took place half a century earlier in the Polish capital.

"When the Rolling Stones played here in 1967, there was a small problem about the fee," he said, with the air of a man setting you up for a delicious punch line. It was early in the tour, when we were standing in front of Poland's tallest building, the 1955 art deco high-rise originally known as the Joseph Stalin Palace of Culture and Science. The bachelor party had wandered off to sprawl on benches and pass around a bottle, while the Spaniards stood staring blankly at the high-rise, waving off my offers to translate for them.

"How did the Rolling Stones come behind the Iron Curtain?" Lucas went on, a twinkle in his eye. "The daughter of First Secretary Wladyslaw Gomulka was a fan, and she pestered and pestered until it was agreed. The concert was of course only for communist party leaders and their families. After, when the Stones received their payment, they go to the bank and find out the money cannot be exchanged or transferred. The money must be used in Poland. They go to the store to buy something, but in those days there is nothing to buy. A few potatoes. Some soap. And vodka. So they bought enough bottles of vodka to fill an entire railroad car. But then they learn the railroad car of vodka also cannot leave Poland. So they donate the vodka to the Polish Artistic Agency. It took them fifty years to drink it all. They drank the last bottle only a year ago."

I have since found variations of this tale on several websites, usually being hotly debated or debunked outright. It's possible nothing Lucas said is true beyond the fact the Stones did play the Joseph Stalin Palace of Culture and Science in 1967. But the story was fun to hear and pass on, which is why Varsovians (as Warsaw residents are known) will probably be retelling it for at least another half century.

If you prefer not to do your sightseeing accompanied by Lithuanian bachelor parties or other disruptive elements, hiring a private guide is often your best option. Read reviews carefully, of course, and make sure you know what's included in the itinerary. There are many sites, such as Rent-a-Guide, Tours by Locals, and Vayable, that organize private tours for a fee. A good guide can illuminate a city, highlighting aspects you'd never discover on your own. Rich and I love a good tour, and while we usually opt for free walking tours that provide a general overview of the history and culture, one of the most enjoyable tours we've ever taken was one booked through Vayable called "When Lisbon was Casablanca."

If you've ever seen the 1942 classic *Casablanca*, you'll remember that just about every character in the film was urgently trying to get to Lisbon, because Portugal remained neutral and its capital was one of the few places in war-ravaged Europe where you could still get passage to the Americas. Our guide, Magda, explained there was much more to it than that. Lisbon prospered during the war years as wealthy refugees, deposed royals, and well-funded spies flooded the economy with cash, jewels, and every other kind of portable asset. Portugal's dictator, António Salazar, didn't want to lose his profitable new guests or get drawn into the war, so he insisted that the various factions coexist in a peaceful manner — or at least not slit each other's throats in public.

"Before Facebook, the cafés were our information exchange," Magda said, gesturing to sidewalk tables on the main square. "Everyone was trying to get a visa, but it was difficult — and very expensive. Everyone hung out here, hoping for news about who could be bribed. Sexy German women claiming to be Swiss were always seducing Allied officers in hopes of getting information from them." As you can imagine, this did nothing to lessen the city's popularity.

One of the last spots on the tour was the Hard Rock Café, housed in the former movie theater where in 1942 *Casablanca* made its Lisbon debut. I tried to imagine what it must have been like to sit in that darkened theater as the famous story began with the narrator's words, "With the coming of the Second World War, many eyes in imprisoned Europe turned hopefully, or desperately, toward the freedom of the Americas. Lisbon became the great embarkation point. But not everybody could get to Lisbon directly, and so a tortuous, roundabout refugee trail sprang up . . ." A trail so many sitting in that theater had taken, although not always through Casablanca.

This is just one sliver of Lisbon's long and colorful history, most of which I know absolutely nothing about. But thanks to the Casablanca Tour, I've started making the acquaintance of this fascinating city. I'm hoping — to steal the closing words of the film — that this is the beginning of a beautiful friendship.

Relationship Lessons from Brain-Enhanced Chimps

Speaking of friendship, I am often asked how Rich and I spend so much time traveling together without getting on each other's nerves, a feat which seems to astonish many of my readers.

"How do you deal with fights with your husband while you're traveling?" one woman asked me during a Q&A session with a British expats' book club in Spain. "You don't write about any arguments in your new book, but there must have been *some*."

It was a fair question. Getting along with others is always a tricky business. And when your journey seems spiraling towards disaster, it's extremely tempting to start hurling blame around, in the misguided belief that doing so will somehow help the situation get back on track.

As it happens, Rich and I are both blessed with easygoing temperaments. But yes, of course, during road trips that can last up to three months, there have been occasional moments of disagreement and discord. Luckily, during our three-plus decades of marriage and visits to more than sixty countries, I've discovered a few useful tricks.

For a start, I've learned that dealing with travel companions requires wisdom that goes beyond what I can glean from self-help books, counselors, psychiatrists, clergy, or even the earthy astuteness of cab drivers and bartenders. No, when I need really profound relationship-saving inspiration, I tend to find it in B-movies, so-so TV shows, and random Facebook comments. Let me give you a few examples that have helped us stay the course in our journey through life.

Late one evening Rich and I were watching an entirely forgettable film about brain-enhanced chimpanzees who were obviously about to outwit the hapless new night watchman. The first time trouble flared, an old hand warned the rookie, "Never let it escalate." Rich and I were immediately struck by the profound wisdom of this. From then on we've made it our policy to deal with any personal conflicts early on, when they're smaller and easier to resolve. We don't wait until our marriage is, metaphorically speaking, overrun with hostile chimpanzee geniuses who have the keys to the weapons cabinet and our car.

Another time we were viewing a rather lackluster 1987 production of a Lord Peter Wimsey mystery. In one scene the famous sleuth made a mildly infelicitous remark to the woman he loved. He instantly retracted it, saying, "I beg your pardon. It was a beastly spasm. Won't happen again." It beautifully defined the moment as a personal lapse, not a reflection of his true sentiments or a policy statement about the nature of their relationship. Nowadays, when one of us utters a cranky remark we know to be unfair and uncalled for, it can be annulled and forgotten simply by saying, "Sorry. Beastly spasm." It's a sort of linguistic "no harm, no foul" ruling that lets us get past a bad moment gracefully.

Then there was the Facebook comment that popped up when I was struggling with a series of unforeseen events that kept delaying our departure on a long-planned three-month railway journey. After I'd posted something bewailing the latest obstacle to our departure, a man I don't even know generously replied with his father's best advice: "Never chase a missed train — get a pastry and wait for the next one." Brilliant! In a crisis, often the only sensible thing to do is regroup over coffee and pastry, or indulge in some other small, pleasurable distraction until you calm down, regain some perspective, and are better prepared to cope.

This goes double when the crisis is your companion's fault. Did you miss the train because *somebody* took too long in the shower or misremembered the schedule? Then you have the high moral ground; don't squander it by throwing a hissy fit. Be nice. Be very, very nice. The other person will feel horribly guilty and strive mightily to do better in the future.

Being in a foreign environment tests all our relationships: familial, friendly, romantic, with strangers, and most of all, with ourselves. It helps to remember that people don't have to be perfect to be convivial comrades, and that luckily, no one in their right mind expects us to be flawless either. And that goes for what we expect of ourselves too. Often we're our own worst critics, giving ourselves harsh mental scoldings for even trivial offenses, such as misreading a map or ordering the wrong dish from an unfamiliar menu. Our faults and imperfections make us who we are, lead us into adventures, and add zip to the journey. Don't be too quick to wish they would disappear.

Oh, the People You'll Meet, the Stories You'll Tell

Like most expats and avid travelers, I enjoy telling stories about all the astonishing things that happen to me abroad, and these tales always center around the people I meet: Martin and Erge, who showed me what it means to live in a truly open society. Johanna with her faux pas among the gypsies. That zany Buddhist monk, who surprised the hell out of me in a way that still makes me chuckle every time I think of him. Lidjia, Mladen, and Doris, who instantly drew me into a warm circle of friendship. There are so many more: the trivia players and zany emcee at Kewl Cat; my fellow survivors of the Cuban airport crisis; the many friends I've met through InterNations. (Except, of course, those young singles in Stockholm!) I'm often asked what I like most about being an expat, and it always comes down to great people.

This time next month or next year, what kinds of stories will you be telling?

I hope you'll be talking about friends you've made and adventures you've shared with congenial companions.

So many memories of overseas adventures are filled with laughter and the simple pleasure of being alive in this vast, crazy, fascinating world, where we keep stumbling over startling differences and finding comfort in the deep similarities that unite us. The poet David Whyte says, "Inside everyone is a great shout of joy waiting to be born." Never be afraid to share your voice with the world. There's no telling who might need to hear it.

Look Inside the Book

DANCING IN THE FOUNTAIN

How to Enjoy Living Abroad

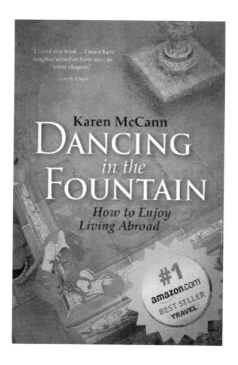

Acclaim for Karen McCann's
DANCING IN THE FOUNTAIN
#1 Amazon Kindle Bestseller in Travel, Spain

"I loved this book. I must have laughed aloud at least once in
every chapter ... The advice in the book is terrific."
Lonely Planet

"Funny and illuminating."
The Local Spain

"A warm, humorous account . . . She makes shopping for a screw
driver sound like a grand adventure."
Rolf Potts, *Vagabonding*

"Karen McCann's engaging style and sense of humor are both
refreshing and immediately evident. In fact, I find
them reminiscent of British author Peter Mayle and his romps in
France, but with a bit more substance."
Spain Expat

"I loved this book. From the very first page the story fizzed with
the energy of possibilities being discussed and plans being made.
This book was an entertaining read, full of wry observations,
dry wit and an acute sense of the ridiculous."
Poly Burns, *Caught Writing*

"McCann's wacky sense of humor will have you smiling on every page."
Rita Golden Gelman, author of *Tales of a Female Nomad*

"I loved *Dancing in the Fountain* for its humor . . . she is definitely one of the best travel writers I have come across."
Vera Marie Badertscher, *A Traveler's Library*

"Her book **is** one long, glorious love letter to the Andalucían capital and its quirky, warm-hearted people."
Maria Foley, *I Was An Expat Wife*

"Of all the expat books I've read, I have to say this is one of the best, rivaling only Peter Mayle's tour de force, *A Year in Provence.* This was my late-afternoon-hammock read recently, and I found myself laughing so uproariously in several spots that I made the hammock sway dangerously and brought my husband and dogs out to see what was going on."
Susanna Perkins, *Future Expats Forum*

"I thoroughly enjoyed immersing myself in the trials and thrills that this American couple experienced after they decided to move to Seville, Spain . . . *Dancing In The Fountain* made me want to put on my dancing shoes and waltz on over to Seville."
Krista Castner, *Luxury Reading*

"*Dancing in the Fountain* is a delightfully well-written true-life adventure story. . . McCann's writing is warm, inviting, immediately charming, and constantly entertaining. Her narrative was so good I found myself wanting to hear more about Cleveland! Now THAT's good travel writing!"
Chris Brady, *New York Times* bestselling author of
A Month of Italy

"*Dancing in the Fountain* is perhaps the best book about travel that I have ever read. It is certainly the best book about living - and living out loud — that I have ever read. It is full of wry humor and it is laugh-out-loud funny — the adventure with the snake, to mention just one . . . "
Guy Thatcher, author of *A Journey of Days*

"Karen McCann's witty, fresh and engaging new book, *Dancing in the Fountain*, captures the charming unpredictability of life in Andalucía. Seen through her eyes, creating a new life in an old European city has never been so delightful, heartwarming and laugh-out-loud funny."
Victoria Twead, *NY Times* bestselling author of
Chickens, Mules and Two Old Fools

PREFACE

When I was growing up, my friends and I used to ask each other, "If you could live anywhere in the world, where would it be?" We'd then spend hours discussing the rival merits of Paris, London, Rome, and anyplace else we could think of that came under the thrilling and glamorous heading of "abroad." Years later, sitting in a dimly lit San Francisco restaurant on my first date with my husband-to-be, the subject came up again. Rich said, "I'd like to live abroad for a year. What do you think about Singapore?" I knew then that he was a keeper.

As it turned out, instead of Singapore, we went to live in Cleveland.

Two weeks after we came back from our honeymoon in the jungles of Costa Rica, a Cleveland firm made Rich an offer no sane person would have refused, and off we went. My sisters were appalled. Our San Francisco friends started referring to us in the past tense and wondering aloud if we'd done something terrible in a past life to deserve our fate. "Costa Rica?" said an old friend of Rich's. "Cleveland? When are you going to stop testing this woman?"

But as it happened, I loved Cleveland (yes, I did!). I had moved around a lot over the years, propelled by fluctuations in the family fortunes and later my own, and I had learned that I could make a good life for myself practically anywhere. One thing I know to be true: the secret is mentally unpacking your bags. Or, as the Buddhists like to put it, being here now.

In my Cleveland days, "here" was an old stone house on a wooded bluff overlooking a river, and "now" was a life filled with interesting work and great friends. We lived twenty-five miles outside the city, in a semirural area with woods, farms, and a large Amish community. We were deep in the American heartland, about as far from "abroad" as you can get.

But Rich always makes good on his promises, and a mere twenty years later, we moved to southern Spain. It began nearly eleven years ago with a visit to a friend's timeshare on the Mediterranean coast, which led to a return visit the following spring to study Spanish. That's when we took a side trip to Seville and found it too intriguing simply to pass through for a couple of days. We spent four spring vacations in Seville, staying for longer and longer periods, until finally we decided to move there "for a year." We've now been living in Seville for six and a half years, in a slightly crumbling old apartment overlooking the sun-bleached tile roof of an eighteenth-century church. A few years back we sold our beloved Cleveland house and bought a cottage in a small town north of San Francisco, near family and longtime friends, to serve as our home base when we're in the US. But most of our time is spent in Seville, and I'm still astonished at my good fortune.

And here's what I've learned: living abroad is easier than you think.

People often say to me, "You have the best of both worlds." (Wistful sigh.) "I wish I could do what you do." Half the time, I know perfectly well that my lifestyle wouldn't suit them at all. They've chosen a different path and are just enjoying the kind of fleeting fantasy that comes with reading about people in wildly different circumstances, like Victorian London or outer space, and trying the idea on for size. After a few seconds, they're only too happy to set aside the fantasy to go back to browsing the Kindle store, helping the kids with their homework, or writing an email to colleagues.

But for anyone who might be seriously interested, I'll just say again, it's easier than you think. Of course, moving abroad — or anywhere, for that matter — has its challenges and will take time and effort to plan and carry out. But you don't have to wait until all the stars are aligned, the dog passes away, your grandkids are all happily married with good jobs, and you win the lottery.

Many people are under the impression that living abroad is terribly expensive — and it can be, if you buy a penthouse in the best neighborhood in Paris or Rome. But if you rent a comfortable apartment in a small, affordable city like Seville, your cost of living may actually go down or, as in our case, remain about the same. Although we pay a bit more in airfares every year, our basic expenses (housing, food, clothing, entertainment, ground transportation) are far more modest in Seville than when we made our home in Cleveland. Among other economies, we live in a walking city and don't need a car to get about. Without the car payments, insurance, garage fees, and maintenance, to say nothing of parking tickets, we can easily afford to hop a bus, rent a car, or take a taxi on those rare occasions when we need to.

Moving abroad may not have to wait until you're retired, either. While not every career can be uprooted and taken with you, I have friends in their twenties, thirties, and forties, often with large dogs and/or small children, who have figured out how to work successfully from a foreign base. In these technologically advanced times, all it takes is a computer to manage projects with business associates, keep tabs on investments, and stay in touch with family and friends in other countries. In fact, between Facebook and other media, I am now more familiar with the minutiae of my loved ones' lives than I was when we lived on the same block or even in the same house. And my initial concerns about missing family and friends evaporated when I learned that when you live in a destination city like Seville, *they* come to *you*. Sometimes the biggest challenge is getting them to leave again — but more about that later.

And contrary to what we've all read in so many charming books about Provence and Tuscany, it turns out that when you move to Europe, you are not actually required to purchase a crumbling old farmhouse in the country and spend years restoring it with the help of semiliterate but wise and amusing locals. That's a great life for some, but I find the country and suburbs to be very isolating, especially in a place like southern Spain, where people are slow to befriend anyone they haven't known since baptism. To me, it's infinitely more agreeable to rent an already-restored apartment in the center of a destination city, where the locals are more open to meeting foreigners and there's a lively and diverse international community. During my twenty years in Ohio, I spent more than enough evenings sitting on the back porch listening to the crickets. Now I'm delighted to be able to stroll around the corner to a flamenco show, wine tasting, or concert any night of the week and go out afterwards to a tapas bar with friends.

While you don't have to be wealthy, retired, or willing to restore a crumbling farmhouse to enjoy living abroad, there are some things you *will* need. The first is a good sense of humor, which is essential to surviving the general upheaval of any major life change, and most especially the social and linguistic pratfalls you'll inevitably be taking. Every foreign language is studded with little trip wires, such as the Spanish word *embarazada*, which sounds so much like the English "embarrassed," but in fact means "pregnant," creating endless opportunities for misunderstandings and faux pas. Or there's the common word *huevos*, literally "eggs" but often used as a slang word for testicles. You'll want to be very careful not to ask the guy at the farmers' market whether he has eggs; he'll inevitably reply "Yes, two big ones," and everyone within earshot will fall about laughing until you flee in confusion and have to find someplace else to buy your breakfast groceries.

An adaptable attitude is also a great help when living abroad. Naturally we all make comparisons with our country of origin, but it's best to avoid constantly demanding that other countries measure up to our standards and norms. I recently read a blog called "A Fantasy About Retiring Abroad," in which a financial planner weighed the pros and cons of living in a foreign country. Her conclusion was that it would be utterly impossible for her (and, she implied, anyone with any sense) to live in Europe because the Europeans do not have a "can-do" attitude and frequently fail to meet American efficiency standards. Oh honey, I wanted to tell her, that's the best reason I can think of *for* living in Europe. It's such a relief to live among people who value other things — such as family, friends, slow-cooked meals, witty and intimate conversation — above optimizing time management. It says a lot about our culture that this financial planner couldn't even have a *fantasy* that failed to achieve productivity benchmarks.

Respect for other cultures is essential too. There are times when all of us find it difficult to let go of preconceived notions of how things ought to work, especially in a foreign business setting. As part of our volunteer work for various organizations assisting struggling microenterprises, in the late 1990s Rich and I went to the former Soviet republic of Georgia. At the end of a fat dossier on the company's issues our case manager advised, "Don't write your report on the plane en route to the assignment." He was so right. One of my first suggestions for our clients was a mail marketing campaign. That's when I discovered that the nation's mail system hadn't functioned since the Soviets pulled out.

"Then how do you send out your bills?" I asked.

"We drive to people's homes. And while the bill collector is inside, the driver spray-paints our phone number on the wall of the building."

"And people don't object to that?" I asked incredulously. In the US there would be a lawsuit filed before the paint was dry.

"No, they like having the number handy." Apparently the phone books and directory assistance service had gone the way of the mail system.

I had to admit it was a great solution. Clearly my clients had a lot to teach me about marketing in the republic of Georgia.

And that's the whole fun of living abroad. You aren't doing things the same old way. You can't. Which means you're going to have to be open to new ways of thinking about *everything*.

Exploring new ways of approaching life can become addictive. "Abroad" is a very big place, and the possibilities are so intriguing that it's often hard to stop browsing and choose where you'd like to live. No matter how comfortably settled we are, Rich can never resist looking at real estate, and he automatically checks out housing prices wherever we travel so he can have the fun of imagining us living there.

"Listen to this," he said once, while reading a newspaper in the Himalayan kingdom of Bhutan. "You can get a three-bedroom house, with garden and toilet, for just four hundred thousand ngultrums. That's less than ten thousand dollars."

Reading the ad over his shoulder, I replied, "Yes, and it's conveniently located in downtown Wangdue Phodrang — which is where exactly?"

Rich had to admit that living in a small market town in central Bhutan might not give us the lifestyle we wanted, even with such bonus extras as garden and toilet.

Before our move to Seville, whenever we saw this kind of alluring real estate deal I would remind Rich of our agreement that we would never seriously consider living anywhere that we hadn't visited three times. We didn't want to make a move we'd repent at leisure. Like most Americans, I grew up on stories of immigrant forebears who left behind everyone and everything they knew forever in order to forge a new life in a new land. I find it immensely comforting to know that today you can try out places before you commit to them, and you can keep your ties to the old country in case things don't work out or just because you enjoy them both.

For me, things did work out. This is the story of why I moved to Seville and how I shaped a new life in a foreign country while maintaining a place for myself in my native land. My story will, I hope, provide you with some ideas about how *you* might experience living abroad in the world, if you ever decide to try it. It *is* possible — fun, even — to engage in a whole new culture, face up to its challenges, and build a life that's truly yours in a country that isn't. And we're lucky enough to live in an age where you can do all that without cutting your ties to your homeland.

This book describes my adventures and misadventures in Seville, but the lessons I've learned can be applied to any international move, whether it's to a bungalow in India, a flat in Moscow, or a *mieszkanie* in Warsaw. I've devoted chapters to the topics that people most often ask me about: learning a foreign language, finding housing, bringing along your beloved pet, making friends, adapting to unfamiliar eating and drinking customs, dealing with a very different health care system, and coping with the arrival of more houseguests than you could ever have imagined possible. The book focuses largely on my experiences in Seville, but you'll also be hearing about my life in the US — in Cleveland and California — to provide context for my stories and to give you a realistic idea of how you, too, might be able to structure a good life that embraces the old as well as the new.

You'll learn about friends I made (some of whom appear here under other names, out of respect for their privacy) and mistakes I blundered into along the way. One of the great things about living abroad is that you have countless new ways to screw up, providing many valuable opportunities for honing your wits and your sense of the ridiculous. We've all read articles about how to keep your brain's synapses firing by doing Sudoku, taking up knitting, or going bird watching, but frankly, I find life in a foreign country to be a far more interesting and effective way to stay sharp. The French writer Émile Zola once said, "If you ask me what I came into the world to do, I will tell you: I came to live out loud." And if you ask me, I will tell you there's nothing quite like going abroad to pump up the volume on your life.

Want to read more?
Dancing in the Fountain: How to Enjoy Living Abroad
is available from Amazon
in paperback and Kindle formats.

And don't miss the next part of our expat exploits,
Adventures of a Railway Nomad:
How Our Journeys Guide Us Home,
which describes our three-month train trip
through Eastern Europe..

Author photo by Rich McCann

ABOUT THE AUTHOR

My checkered past includes working as a journalist, editor, graphic designer, corporate communications director, marketing consultant, and copywriter in Cleveland, California, and Boston. When my husband, Rich, took early retirement, we began volunteering as business consultants to struggling microenterprises in emerging and post-war nations in Africa, Central America, the Caucasus region, and Eastern Europe.

During our 32 years of marriage we've visited more than 60 countries together, and of all those places, Seville is the one that kept calling us back. Vacations there grew longer and longer until in 2004 we decided to make it our home "for a year." We're still there and still in love with the city. We also make regular visits back to the States, because America is something you have to stay in practice for, and we don't want to lose our touch.

When we reached our sixties, Rich and I began to wonder whether we could still have the kind of spontaneous travel adventures we'd enjoyed in our youth, so we set off to find out. One August morning, we walked out of our Seville apartment and strolled to the train station with small, roll-aboard bags, a Eurail pass, and a railway map of Europe. With no reservations, no fixed time limit, and only a loose idea of an itinerary, we spent three months riding the rails, mostly through Eastern Europe. The results of this and other journeys became two bestselling travel memoirs, three guides, and a host of blog posts, interviews, and articles. My travel tips and adventure stories have appeared in *Huffington Post, International Living Magazine, New York Daily News, Los Angeles Times*, and *Lonely Planet*.

And here's what I've learned: No! You absolutely do *not* have to settle for boring, predictable travel at any age. In fact, you don't have to settle for a boring, predictable life either. If, like me, you spent your childhood secretly longing to live overseas, maybe this is the time to start thinking seriously about how much you might enjoy moving abroad.

Karen McCann

**CAFÉ
SOCIETY
PRESS**

Hartland & Co.

1100 Superior Avenue East, Suite 700

Cleveland, OH 44114

For more on Karen McCann's books

visit her Amazon author page and her website

EnjoyLivingAbroad.com

Printed in Great Britain
by Amazon